FAITH, LOVE, AND HUMAN TRAFFICKING
The Story of Karola de la Cuesta

Raquel A. Caspi, PHD

TRILOGY

Trilogy Christian Publishers

A Wholly Owned Subsidary of Trinity Broadcasting Network

2442 Michelle Drive

Tustin, CA 92780

For information, address Trilogy Christian Publishing

Rights Department, 2442 Michelle Drive, Tustin, Ca 92780.

Trilogy Christian Publishing/ TBN and colophon are trademarks of Trinity Broadcasting Network.

For information about special discounts for bulk purchases, please contact Trilogy Christian Publishing.

10 9 8 7 6 5 4 3 2 1

Library of Congress Cataloging-in-Publication Data is available.

ISBN 979-8-89333-369-5

ISBN 979-8-89333-368-8 (ebook)

DEDICATION

To the victims of human trafficking and abuse, and to every soul who has endured unspeakable suffering: you are not alone. Your resilience in the face of unimaginable adversity is an inspiration of hope and courage to us all.

To the countless individuals who have extended a helping hand, offering solace, support, and sanctuary to those in need: you are the unsung heroes of our communities. Your compassion and generosity have helped heal wounds and restore faith in humanity.

This book is for you—all of you—who have turned pain into purpose and darkness into light.

ACKNOWLEDGMENTS

We acknowledge every single person who has been part
of this journey. You know who you are, and we are
eternally grateful for your love and support.

DISCLAIMER

Although the publisher and the author have made every effort to ensure that the information in this book was correct at press time, and while this publication is designed to provide accurate information in regard to the subject matter covered, the publisher and the author assume no responsibility for errors, inaccuracies, omissions, or any other inconsistencies herein and hereby disclaim any liability to any party for any loss, damage, or disruption caused by errors or omissions, whether such errors or omissions result from negligence, lack of information, or any other cause.

This work depicts actual events in the life of Karola De la Cuesta as truthfully as recollection permits. While all persons within are actual individuals, names have been changed to respect their privacy.

TABLE OF CONTENTS

FOREWORD

Since 2007, I have crossed paths with countless human trafficking survivors and numerous families with missing daughters. From 2009 to 2012, I spearheaded Mexico's Anti-Trafficking Law to bring perpetrators like those who harmed Karola and her family to justice. Regrettably, in today's world, a disturbing number of children vanish each day, with impunity on the rise due to insufficient law enforcement not just in Mexico but globally.

Encountering Karola and listening to her family's quest for justice in Mexico, the USA, Spain, and Brazil is deeply troubling. It epitomizes the most heinous forms of labor exploitation, forced labor, slavery, and sexual exploitation, all shielded by politicians and an industry that has twisted these crimes into a widespread culture across nations. Despite enduring these horrors, the first time I heard the harrowing accounts of her experiences, I was moved to tears. It is remarkable that Karola's book emanates love and stands as a beacon for prevention, justice, and truth, devoid of bitterness but filled with forgiveness.

The anguish that Karola's parents and sisters endured, not knowing the fate of their daughters for two years, mirrors the hell experienced by thousands of parents in Mexico. Recent statistics from REDIM (Network for Children's Rights) and the National Registry of Missing and Unlocated Persons (RNPDNO) portray a disturbing reality, with a total of 16,999 missing children in Mexico as of March 11, 2024.

This book will play a crucial role in unveiling the depths of malevolence and manipulation that traffickers employ. Any parent could fall prey to these traps without proper awareness. Today, social platforms lurk for vulnerable minors, and reading this book will equip them to identify perilous grooming signs.

Karola, now a commendable mother of two young individuals with faith and entrepreneurial aspirations, has triumphed over adversity and continual revictimization by society and authorities for over two decades. Despite this, she leads a life filled with spiritual abundance and joy bestowed by God.

Karola's narrative will inspire readers with her faith, resilience, and love. It will empower at-risk youth to recognize danger signals, urge authorities to uphold the law, and embolden parents to safeguard their children. Raquel Caspi, the author of this book, draws upon her expertise as a psychologist and years of aiding survivors to narrate Karola's tale of resilience and triumph.

Karola's journey epitomizes successful reintegration, showcasing the transformative power of Christ in recovery and sustained success. This book serves as a clarion call for society to unite and support all victims of human trafficking and exploitation.

I vividly recall the assembly of nearly thirty civil society organizations in Washington in May 2023, where Cindy Jacobs had just concluded a prayer session for us. The inception of this book by the Kaleido executive board the following day, inspired by Karo's testimony, remains etched in my memory.

Karola shines as a beacon of hope and deserves love, support, understanding, and apologies from authorities, media, and society as a whole. This book, born from Karola's testimony, aims to illuminate the darkest corners of human trafficking and exploitation, showcasing the resilience and faith of the bravest survivor: Karola.

—Rosi Orozco.

PREFACE

Beloved Readers,

I, Karola, stand before you at the precipice of unveiling fragments of my life's narrative. In this rare instance within the pages of this book, I extend a direct address to you. My purpose is twofold: firstly, to convey the profound gratitude residing in my heart towards God and each of you for cradling this book in your hands, and secondly, to express a broader appreciation for life's entirety, as it grants me the privilege to share pivotal themes that resonate deeply within my being.

This journey began a couple of years ago, germinating from a latent desire to find the courage to tell my story. Uncertain of the specifics, my initial pledge to myself birthed the notion of a book entitled *We Need to Talk*. This proposal sprang from my immersion in the realm of human rights organizations, survivor narratives, and personal experiences. It became evident that many societal ills could be thwarted if only we possessed genuine awareness of prevailing circumstances and risks. Real and meaningful information, open dialogue, and the collective effort to foster communication channels for prevention and support emerged as the pillars of my emergent endeavor.

In traversing the years, countless women and, on occasion, men, survivors of abuse, have entrusted me with the sacred unveiling of their stories. Their narratives, whispered as if releasing long-guarded secrets, often carry refrains of self-doubt, "It wasn't worth disclosing," or "Why speak out when no one will believe?" Grateful for their trust, I have come to recognize the imperative need for enhanced avenues of liberation and healing. It is an acknowledgment that transcends the individual and beckons us towards a collective commitment to a more harmonious existence.

Silence, I have observed, cloaks abuse in a shroud of convenience. Conversely, divulging the truth emerges as the most potent weapon against perpetuation. Sharing one's experience, unburdened by the weight of pain, with the right support and divine guidance, becomes a cathartic journey toward liberation and eventual healing.

This endeavor, however noble in theory, requires a formidable dose of courage. A courage demanded not only of me but of every activist who has weathered the storms of criminality. The act of narrating one's story

3

becomes a precarious tightrope walk, inviting the specter of re-victim-ization, judgment, vulnerability, and a haunting revisit to the darkest corners of our existence. Despite the global resonance of the #MeToo movement, its intrinsic efficacy is far from universal. It stands as a beacon on paper, yet its illumination is sporadic in our hearts, cultures, legal systems, and daily lives.

My personal trajectory, extending back over two decades, predates the emergence of this movement. In those years, the act of disclosure not only incurred the wrath of my abusers, authorities, and circumstances but was met with societal exclusion. According to statistics, victims hesitate to report, compelled by familial pressures to maintain silence in a misguided bid to shield loved ones. Yet, amidst the terror of those years, a fellow survivor proclaimed, "I will report, for God declares, 'The truth will set you free.'" In hindsight, it wasn't just physical freedom we craved, but mental and emotional liberation. Speaking out, guided by divine promises such as "Do not be afraid; keep on speaking, do not be silent" and "The Lord loves justice and righteousness," became an imperative rooted in faith, transcending the temporal boundaries of societal norms.

It was through the intercession of Rosi Orozco, an indefatigable activist, that the path to my revelation unfolded. God, utilizing her as an instrument, led me to Raquel Caspi, a luminous soul and astute psychologist and author, with whom I shared an immediate resonance regarding the purpose of this book. Together, we amalgamated our perspectives, experiences, and visions into a tapestry that transcends the contours of my individual story. This narrative is not solely mine; it encapsulates the collective experiences of countless souls who, in the shadows of anonymity, share parallel tales of resilience.

As this odyssey unfolds, I extend an invitation. In moments where the narrative grows arduous or emotionally taxing, summon your own reservoirs of courage and persevere. Faith burgeons within me, affirming that this book has found its way into your hands for a purpose—a purpose that transcends individual boundaries, beckoning us to comprehend and nurture one another more fervently. Our stories, whether cloaked in victimhood or not, converge into a symphony of survival, imploring us to foster understanding and vigilant care. Let us equip ourselves with the wisdom to react appropriately, to support those in peril, and to stand as pillars of strength for the afflicted.

PREFACE

This endeavor transcends the dichotomy of "good" and "bad." It is a clarion call to surmount barriers, cultural biases, societal taboos, religious preconceptions, and the pervasive cloak of ignorance. Let us, gradually and consciously, dismantle the edifice of toxic behaviors, both within ourselves and in others. While acknowledging the sincerity of our efforts, let us strive for a loftier standard—for ourselves, our progeny, our families, and our cherished friends.

To each of you who delves into these pages, absorbing the essence of these words, I extend profound gratitude. May you, if you so choose, become torchbearers of the imperative dialogue encapsulated within these pages.

With heartfelt appreciation,
Karola.

PROLOGUE

In the late 1990s, a shockwave rippled through Mexico and other parts of the world as the Interpol announced a breakthrough in a high-profile case involving a pop singer and her manager, both of whom had been on the run from authorities. The revelation stunned the public, shedding light on the dark underbelly of exploitation within the entertainment industry. Among the grim discoveries was the rescue of numerous young women held captive under the guise of promises of stardom.

All of the survivors were reduced to mere fodder for public consumption. One of them, a seventeen-year-old girl at the time of her liberation, was rescued with her six-month-old baby in her arms—a baby that was procreated through rape from the manager that was forty-four years old at the time—yet had become her testament of faith, love, and hope. Having been cut off from the outside world for years and enduring unimaginable suffering, her spirit battered but never broke. Little did she imagine the media frenzy surrounding the case and how it would take a toll...exacerbating the challenges she faced in rebuilding her life. Caught in the crossfire of sensationalism, she found herself thrust into the spotlight against her will, her identity reduced to a mere footnote in a narrative crafted by others for their own benefit, where the relentless pursuit of sensational stories overshadowed her humanity. Yet, amid the chaos, she found solace in her faith and began to reclaim her narrative.

One would think that after more than two decades, the media circus would have gradually faded into obscurity, yet it is not so. Through this book, this woman reclaims her narrative and tells her story, one that is a journey marked by faith, resilience, courage, and unwavering commitment to reclaiming her voice. Though the scars of her past may never fully fade, she emerged from the shadows stronger and more determined than ever, taking to activism and advocacy to become a voice for the voiceless. Her journey serves as a reminder of the resilience of the human spirit and the enduring power of faith in the face of darkness. This is the story of Karola de la Cuesta.

INTRODUCTION

Every book has many chapters. Although different from one another, they are intertwined to explain the big picture. Life works like that as well. When we are submerged in one of the chapters, sometimes we have difficulty looking forward, and at times, it's even harder looking back. We are immersed in what is currently happening. But like with every chapter, every event is temporary, although it might not feel that way at the time.

For some of us, there comes a certain time in our lives when we reflect on our most difficult and darkest moments and wonder how it is that we are still standing. We look back and wonder how we found our strength, where it came from, and what it has allowed us to overcome.

Other times, we might wonder what the source of that strength is and where and who we would be without the experiences that contributed to building the person we are today.

The answers I have encountered both through research as well as throughout my career as a psychologist usually involve love, faith, and hard internal work. Yet, every story is different.

This is a story about love, resilience, and unwavering faith. It is also a story about human trafficking.

Welcome, dear readers, to a story that I hope will inspire you as much as it has inspired me.

CHAPTER 1:
A Godsent Friendship

I met Karola at ███████ in Arlington, Virginia. A beautiful place where different influential people have met throughout decades to discuss important matters. I am a board member of Kaleido, an NGO against human trafficking whose mission is to journey with survivors of modern slavery on their path to recovery and freedom.

As I was sitting in the second row of chairs organized in a semicircle, knowing it would soon be time to introduce myself to a group of about forty strangers, I took a deep breath. Despite the many times I have spoken publicly, I always get the same feeling throughout my body, and the same thoughts bounce around my head. *Breathe in, breathe out. Inhale for four seconds, hold your breath for four seconds, and exhale for four seconds.* Hoping I wouldn't blush the moment I stood up in front of so many extraordinary people; I could feel my mouth completely dry. *Ugh! I hope my voice doesn't crack*, I thought.

I introduced myself fairly eloquently and tried to look around the room as I spoke; I could feel the blood rushing to my face.... *Why can't I get this under control?* I thought as my mouth kept talking.

"Hello, everyone. I am Raquel. I am a transpersonal psychologist with a PhD in human development who has therapeutically supported human trafficking survivors in their rehabilitation and journey toward mental health. My doctoral investigation was about resilience and the meaning of life after human trafficking. I have found that human beings are so remarkable that we can go through the worst of times and learn to find our way back to peace."

I didn't know what else to say. I'm not a fan of public speaking, let alone English. Although it is my first language, it is not the language I have spoken the most throughout my life. I was born and raised in Mexico City as the daughter of a Mexican father and an American mother, and then moved to Colorado when I was forty years old. I have absolutely no accent when I speak, but I'm still getting the hang of translating my ideas as I do.

So many astonishing, extraordinary people here, I thought. *What am I doing here?*

Impostor syndrome...not a fun sidekick.

As the hours went by and I heard everyone introduce themselves, I was feeling even smaller. I'm just a therapist. I don't even have my license here yet (because, curiously enough, if you don't study in the US, validating your credentials is a complete nightmare).

I don't write policies, I'm not "important," nobody has ever even heard of me, and I still don't understand how I am part of this extraordinary group of people having such important conversations about human trafficking. Lucky? Definitely. Professional? Of course. Experienced? Without a doubt. Good enough to be sitting in this room with such remarkable people? Not in my head.

As the day went by, I could feel my stomach rumbling...I was on EST, a two-hour difference, and all my stomach managed to deal with at 6 a.m. my time (when I woke up) was coffee. It was now much later, and I realized I was starving. Luckily, our lunch break, which was also at this beautiful venue, was just minutes away.

There were so many people that we couldn't all fit into one table, so there were two large ones. One where we were having our meeting and another in a room upstairs. *I'll just stay down here*, I thought...not that it makes a difference, but I get extremely overstimulated being around many people.

So, I stayed downstairs, picked a chair at the corner of the table, and sat down. I'm an extroverted introvert. I do extremely well in social situations, yet I get exhausted easily. I knew I was going to "have" to engage in conversation during lunch, but all I really wanted was to go outside and walk around this gorgeous place to ground myself with a little nature.

Yet, I was the first to sit down at a large empty table, not making much eye contact to see who would sit beside me, hoping to finally get some food in my system and then get back to the meeting. Little did I know the plans that awaited.

Just like every other person there, Karola introduced herself when it was her turn. A human trafficking survivor from Mexico who had been through hell and back. I had heard about her briefly growing up; it was a huge scandal involving public figures. I was about seventeen years old when it all happened, and I was extremely consumed by my own drama. I remember looking at her as she eloquently spoke in English, thinking she was extremely beautiful.

Not to be a total grinch, but having heard so many horrible stories of the different women I have supported therapeutically, I don't get scared easily. Apparently, after the initial shock of emotionally getting into the world of human trafficking (mind you, the initial shock took about a year and a lot of therapy), my heart developed some type of armor.

Anyway, back to the story. Karola obviously did not get into details about her story, and as an activist, she was there to see how she could be of help.

Curiously enough, we ended up sitting together during lunch. The chicken salad that was served with croissants looked delicious, even for a vegetarian...that's when I realized how hungry I really was at that point. I got a plate with no chicken, and then, Karola asked the person who was serving us if she could have the same thing I was having.

I instantly asked her, "Are you a vegetarian, too?" That was our first interaction.

She looked at me and simply said, "Not really. I just don't eat chicken. During the years I was held captive, they would feed me mostly fruit peels, egg shells, and burnt chicken fat." She said it nonchalantly, not expecting a reaction from me, just being honest. I loved her for that.

"That is just horrible," I said, and just like if I was talking to an old friend about any topic, the conversation flowed non-stop.

We talked about spirituality, faith, and therapy. It was a gift; I hate small talk. And before we knew it, lunchtime was over, and our meeting was back on track.

After this beautiful reunion of like-minded individuals with similar goals, I was exhausted from the social interaction. For sure, this has always been the case for me, but after a year and four months of lockdown due to COVID-19 in Mexico, my social battery has lost even more of its power. I was ready to head back to my hotel and disconnect to reconnect to myself.

"We are going out to get these amazing cupcakes," Karola told me. "Want to come along?"

Although I really wanted to continue talking to her, I was depleted, so I answered with the same honesty she had answered me with before. "I get extremely overstimulated after being with a lot of people," I said. "I really need to decompress."

She smiled and said, "I totally get it. Let's exchange numbers, and in case you are up for it, text me later."

"Sounds like a plan," I said.

I called an Uber, and as I waited, we talked a little more. I asked her how old she was; she looked so young to me.

"I'm forty, I'm from '82."

"So am I! What month?"

And just like that, after honest, genuine interactions, we ended up having amazing small talk about being forty years old and skin care routines. Then, my Uber got there, and I went to my hotel.

I didn't text her. I was exhausted. Yet, without knowing I would, I saw her the following morning. It was our board meeting; she showed up to touch base with the extraordinary friend we have in common before heading out to a museum.

"Touching base" turned into something else. A beautiful conversation that ended in prayer, and then, the light bulb went off.

"Raquel can write your story," our amazing friend and colleague said to her.

I looked at her and smiled. "I would love to."

I truly believe that to be in the right place at the right time is to be a participant in a divine plan.

I sent her the book I wrote in 2021 about the story of a Mexican human trafficking survivor I have supported therapeutically, asked her to read it so she could get an idea of the way I write, and told her, "Take your time. Feel free to explore all the options you want; there is absolutely no pressure."

She responded to my text with a heart emoji, and we all traveled the same day to different locations. We got in touch a couple of weeks later, and being 2594 miles apart, we had our first virtual meeting. It lasted three hours, and during this time, we didn't once talk about her story. We talked about life, love, motherhood, children, faith.... It felt like we were old friends.

CHAPTER 1: A GODSENT FRIENDSHIP

"We have to stay on the ball on our next meeting," I told her...but it would actually take three more meetings of more than three hours each to start talking about what happened to her in the late 1990s.

The details she shared with me about everything that happened to her at such an early age were terrifying. Everything she went through was a complete and total nightmare that I would never wish upon any living being. The legal documents she shared with me, her witness statement, pictures.... I can't begin to explain how my armored heart was crushed, but I can tell you the exact moment it did; it was during our fourth conversation.

"Raquel, imagine being seventeen years old and having gone through everything except what every normal person experiences. I had traveled the world, had a baby, been raped, been abused psychologically and physically, been obligated to perform forced labor, been away from my parents for years, been coerced, been alienated, been starved, been locked in a room with no food or water for days, been transported into another country illegally, and above all, didn't have the opportunity to experience the amazing 'firsts' most people have by age seventeen. I never had a consensual first kiss, or a graduation, or a first love. I was deprived of absolutely every normal thing every human should experience, which was replaced by torture."

This shook me to my core. We are exactly the same age, we are from the same country, and we have so many similarities it continues to surprise us every time we talk...and yet, Karola had experienced the unimaginable at the same age I was crying over my first heartbreak. She didn't experience this because her parents didn't take care of her or because she brought it on herself (which clearly is an absurd thing to think, yet when it comes to women experiencing so many different types of abuse, something I've heard way too many times). She experienced this because this can happen to absolutely anybody, with no exceptions.

Human trafficking, exploitation, abuse, trauma...this can happen to anybody. Traffickers don't discriminate. It doesn't matter if you are rich or poor, male or female, young or old, educated or uneducated, or have a functional or dysfunctional family dynamic.... It is a business, the second most lucrative illegal activity worldwide.

So, here we are, dear readers, about to embark on a journey where your hearts will be crushed while remaining hopeful. This book has several objectives, one of which is to tell Karola's story. Others are intrinsically intertwined to inform, educate, and sensitize about human trafficking. My favorite, if I dare be so bold, is to address the beautiful effect faith and love can have on resilience and how Karola is the perfect example of this. I have included some of Karola's favorite Bible verses because faith is the primary reason she is still standing.

So, now that you know how it all began, let's get started.

CHAPTER 2:
Human Trafficking

When I began working therapeutically with human trafficking survivors, something inside me changed. This internal shift put me in a place, emotionally, I had never been before, and as my innocence and ignorance died, I was reborn as a completely different person. The process was long and difficult like most transformational processes tend to be. At first, I couldn't understand how slavery still exists, and not only that, but that it is the second most lucrative illegal activity worldwide.

Working with people requires connection; obviously, that's something we already know, but even though we know it, we tend to forget the importance of really connecting, really listening...and this is with other people as well as with ourselves. To learn who we are behind the mask and to do this requires an abysmal amount of vulnerability and empathy.

So, when I started working with survivors of human trafficking, I got to experience a side of myself, particularly my vulnerability and empathy, which I had never experienced before. How was I supposed to put myself in these women's shoes?

But I tried...and I did, and in doing so, by really connecting with my vulnerability and empathy, I went to the extreme. I made these situations my own. During the first months, my general disappointment with the human race reached its limit, months in which I, being a person who trusts any human being, began to distrust everyone around me. Why? Because I had never been in contact with that part of me.

What happened? As a good therapist, I worked on it in therapy. And I understood that the background of most of the symptoms that I was acting out towards my loved ones revolved around fear.

Fear is actually a wonderful thing because fear warns us—that is its function. Fear is found in the limbic system of the brain, specifically in the amygdala, and what happens is that it still works as it did when we lived in caves. Fear is at the service of the preservation of the species... and it warns us, with the same intensity that it did when a mammoth was getting close, that a car cut us off in traffic.

But since this is no longer so functional for us, as we are surrounded by other kinds of fears, it often happens that our fear is disguised as stress and anxiety. And that generates anger. That was what I experienced: anxiety and stress due to the fear generated through the experiences of others.

Something I found was that although the experiences of these women deeply touched my heart and connected me with my own vulnerability and empathy, they were not my own. In order to help them, I had to take two steps back emotionally, integrate my feelings, take care of myself, and be professional. Like the typical example of the airplane: if there is depressurization, first we have to put on the oxygen mask, and then we will be able to help others put theirs on. If we try to help others before helping ourselves, we may run out of oxygen, and then no one gets out alive.

I can be empathic when connecting, but the moment I make others' situations my own, I can no longer be objective. And if I'm not objective, what good comes out of all of my knowledge and experience?

There is a saying in Spanish I absolutely love, and constantly use. Literally translated, it says, "In a blacksmith's house, a wooden mattock," and here, there was not going to be a wooden mattock. In Mexico, these women generally do not have psychological help, and if they do, it is for a period of three months.

Can you imagine getting out of something like this in three months? A real therapeutic process cannot be given in a predetermined period, and even if it could, three months is ridiculous. So, I understood that I had to deal with my feelings to help these women, or I had to say goodbye to them. I dealt with my feelings.

I realized that working with these women led me to question many things, among them, the possibilities that women have, in this case, Mexican women, to get ahead in a macho, misogynistic, and retrograde country. Seeing the injustices, especially towards women, makes me exceedingly angry. Yet, anger is also an extraordinary emotion if we learn how to regulate it, and one of its functions is to set limits. But what real limits can I genuinely set towards these inhumane, mind-blowing, extreme injustices?

At first, I was struck by the fact that while I may have had much better opportunities than some of them did, thanks to my socio-cultural and socio-economic status, at the end of the day, I was just a woman in a country dominated by misogynistic men, and then I understood something else. I am not just one woman; we are many. And therein lies the strength. So, despite the reality that is lived in Mexico (and all over the world. I must say, Mexico is a country of origin, transit, and destiny for human trafficking, and responsible for 70 percent of the distribution of child pornography), I will continue to put one foot in front of the other for this cause, and I am not alone.

So, as you can imagine, despite having my empathy "regulated" and my fears and anger identified...many times, it still continues to be complicated. So, I've also worked a lot internally on trying to turn it around, obviously, to the greatest extent possible, with these realities.

There is fear, pain, injustice, impotence, and anger, but there is also hope and resilience. My PhD research was about the meaning of life and resilience in survivors of human trafficking. My objective was to understand the meaning of life and resilience survivors developed from the perspective of logotherapy. Logotherapy is the philosophical and therapeutic theory developed by Viktor Frankl, the psychiatrist who wrote *Man's Search for Meaning* after having survived the Holocaust.

Something that seems extraordinary to me is the ability that human beings have to survive emotionally. Seriously, think about it: how many things, no matter how painful, have you overcome? And honestly, no one has shown me that better than the survivors of human trafficking I have had the privilege and honor to get to know. Luna is one of them. A woman with a story worth sharing, for which I gave myself the task of doing it in the book *La Estrella de Luna*. Writing this book was one of the greatest challenges I have ever had. I felt such a great responsibility to communicate this reality. I needed to talk about what was happening in Mexico, but I had to do it with respect and without morbid details to give Luna the place she deserved. Although writing it was somewhat therapeutic for me, I knew that many would not want to read it.

Even very close people told me, "I'm going to buy it because I know the royalties go to the cause, but I'm not going to read it." And although that made me very angry (apparently everything makes me angry), I had to understand that, for some, it's easier not to know what's going on.

It is a difficult subject to write about and difficult to read about. It is a subject that is literally all around us because human trafficking not only covers sexual exploitation, but it has many modalities, including forced labor or involuntary servitude. But we don't see it, and it's not because we are bad people but because we have already normalized it without actually realizing it. The thing is, by normalizing, we become indifferent and continue to live in a bubble of false security that gives us a feeling of comfort that we don't want to leave, and I get it, but that's not how things change. Things change when we are empathetic (to normal degrees) because from empathy, we cannot be indifferent; empathy fuels connection.

Without understanding how, the book was selected among 5,200 others and was one of the five finalists for the 2021 Amazon Storyteller Award.[1] I had never imagined in my entire life that this would happen. The book didn't win, but it did shake the readers, which was always one of my goals, and it shook them to the point of Amazon making a donation to the NGO of my preference that works with human trafficking survivors.

This, in my opinion, is what happens when we connect with our empathy. We help and contribute from wherever we are because empathy helps us to really connect to others and encourages us to be resilient, transform, and generate change.

My first session with Luna was very difficult. I know you're thinking: *Well, obviously....* Yes, but not because of what you think.

One of the first things Luna told me was, "I don't believe in psychologists; I've been my own psychologist for nine years, and I don't trust women."

Luna was kidnapped together with her cousin when they were leaving the annual festival in her town and transported in the back of a trailer from the State of Mexico to Puebla to be sold for a hundred dollars to a couple who would be in charge of sexually exploiting them. The person who was cruelest to her during the unimaginable hell she went through was Yazmin, her madam.

She lost her virginity to twenty-three men on the first night they exploited her; she was fourteen years old. She was denied clean drinking water, beaten to the point of immobilization, and only allowed three hours of sleep per night. For a studious middle school teenager who wanted to be a lawyer when she grew up, everything changed in a matter of seconds.

---

1   Amazon KDP. "Premio Literario Amazon Storyteller 2021 Ceremonia." YouTube, November 17, 2021. https://www.youtube.com/watch?v=C0-EGZ4vFIE.

CHAPTER 2: HUMAN TRAFFICKING

Her dreams disintegrated hour by hour, while her work days (seven days a week) consisted of twelve hours of dancing in her underwear, hair and makeup to look more attractive, but not older, to attract clients who paid to rape her. The remaining nine hours consisted of cleaning the floors, tables, rooms, and bathrooms of the place where she had to be forcefully for approximately fifteen days. After that time, the place would change, but her job remained the same.

While her family was looking for her in bars, tolerance zones, ravines, rivers, and hospitals in the State of Mexico, Morelos, and Puebla, the fourteen-year-old girl was forced to sell her body to pay for another day of life. Her story is one of millions about human trafficking, yet one who, due to her bravery and strength, was able to escape (twice), the second time succeeding and becoming part of the 2 percent of victims that actually survive.

If you don't know much about human trafficking (I didn't until I did), something that blew my mind is that there are 40.3 million victims of modern slavery worldwide[2] and that women and girls are disproportionately vulnerable to modern slavery, accounting for 71 percent of all victims.

I met Luna almost ten years after she lived through hell, and during our time together in her therapeutic process, she changed her mind about psychologists. I honestly think she changed her mind because we worked as a team because, more than sharing her story with me, as she has done in many interviews over the years, she was able to bond with me enough to tell me what really happened to her—internally. We learned so much from each other, and also, the truth is, we share the same sarcastic sense of humor, which meant that many times, we ended up having very pleasant conversations about many other things that have nothing to do with what happened to her. She taught me, among so many valuable life lessons, that being a victim of human trafficking was only one of the many, many things that made her who she was.

After getting to know Luna in-depth, I understood many things. To begin with, what resilience really means. Being resilient does not mean being resistant; it means finding the internal resources to transform the pain of what has happened to us and move forward. I love to explain resilience this way: the old buildings in Mexico City, the ones downtown, for

---

2   "Global Slavery Index." Walk Free, n.d. https://www.globalslaveryindex.org/.

example, are very strong. They have solid foundations and are made of quality materials—no drywall—but at the time of an earthquake, they do not have shock absorbers, they cannot move with the unexpected, they are not flexible...they shatter because they can't move. No matter how strong we are or how strong we think we are, if we don't develop the ability to be flexible to transform our pain, we break into a thousand pieces.

Resilience does not come from denying what happens to us or making it smaller because there are worse things. It happens through a process, one that, among so many things, involves feeling it, crying it out, mourning what once was, dealing with it, accepting it...and then wiping away our tears, putting on mascara, and putting one foot in front of the other.

And as women, if we start to dig a little deeper, despite our opportunities, or lack thereof, we tend to put one foot in front of the other, hoping that our actions, no matter how small they may feel, help others.

The fundamental point of resilience is to transform, to continue advancing. It's not staying in pain; it's finding a way to keep moving forward, even though some days it seems like getting out of bed is a challenge. And the beauty of resilience is that, collectively, it's a great weapon for battle. As individuals, we live it, but when we can go through it in a shared experience with others, it is a gift because we are supported and because resilience leads us to see difficulties as opportunities. Resilience is shifting from judgment to compassion within ourselves and with others.

As women, we continue to move forward. In the US, the Nineteenth Amendment, passed in 1924, "guaranteed" women's right to vote after years of hard work from activists. It doesn't come as a surprise, however, that many women of color were excluded when the Nineteenth Amendment was signed into law, and obviously, the ongoing battle for true equality continues to be extremely complex. In Mexico, women had the right to vote in 1953.

When, at some point, I discussed this with my children some years ago, they were both very surprised. It was my son's response that fascinated me, though, "I don't understand. Why?" He wasn't angry, he wasn't outraged, he just genuinely didn't understand why. And I smiled. Because that, to me, meant we have really made progress. At least I can proudly say, being Mexican-American, that there is no macho blood running in this household.

We continue moving forward because we are discovering and learning to integrate our femininity without replicating masculinity—more specifically, the machismo or micro-machismo that we also have as women. We are moving forward because we have realized we can embrace empathy, which connects us authentically, encouraging us to unite. The beauty of us humans is that united, we can change the world. Having strong bonds encourages us to be resilient and gives us one more reason to keep going. By coming together, we collaborate...we stop competing with each other, and by teaming up, the truth is that we have achieved the unimaginable. When we genuinely understand that we are all in this together, something inside shifts.

In my experience with human trafficking survivors who managed to escape or were rescued in Mexico, it is the women who manage the shelters. The women are the ones who take care of them every day and night, the ones who educate them, teach them, love them, and make them food. To see this up close, to meet the girls in the shelters (five- through sixteen-year-old girls who were rescued from slavery and exploitation), and to see all the women who every day (and the nights that are the hardest) take care of them so lovingly that they remind them to put cream on after they take a shower, fills my heart with hope. Because we understand that we need each other, we connect with others and with each other to help those who need it in any way possible. That is what I decided to take from my experience with human trafficking survivors. Not the horror, the grief, the anger, and the disillusion, but the hope, the love, and the connection that can happen when human beings decide to help each other survive and get better.

Even with an estimated 27.6 million victims worldwide at any given time, human trafficking is not merely the second most lucrative illegal business worldwide. It is not confined to a global crime that trades in people of all genders, ages, and backgrounds and exploits them for profit. That generally takes two forms: sex trafficking, in which a commercial sex act is induced by force, fraud, or coercion, or in which the person induced to perform such act has not attained eighteen years of age; or the recruitment, harboring, transportation, provision, or obtaining of a person for labor or services, through the use of force, fraud, or coercion for the purpose of subjection to involuntary servitude, peonage, debt bondage, or slavery.[3]

---

3   "Human Trafficking." ICE, n.d. https://www.ice.gov/features/human-trafficking.

Human trafficking is also the story of "I," a five-year-old girl from Veracruz who, following the academic setbacks caused by the pandemic, attended evening tutoring classes where the "teachers" tortured her in order to extract her blood and obtain adrenochrome. Adrenochrome is a derivative of oxidized adrenaline that the body metabolizes in high-stress and terror situations. Some people believe that consuming it produces a sensation surpassing that of consuming mescaline. "I" was also forced, along with other children, to undress and engage in sexual acts that were recorded and sold.

Human trafficking also includes the story of "E," a nineteen-year-old who, while at a bar with her boyfriend, left her drink unattended and later began to feel nauseous and lose control of her body. She went to the bathroom and lost consciousness. She was sold and sexually abused. They call it "express trafficking," and it involves approaching the person in charge, pointing out anyone in the establishment, paying a certain amount to have their drink tampered with, and then sexually abusing an unconscious person in the bathroom.

Human trafficking also includes the story of "N," a ten-year-old boy who, due to not selling enough candies at the traffic lights to meet a daily quota of ten dollars, was mercilessly beaten by his homeless parents. "N" was run over and lost a leg while desperately trying to meet his daily quota.

Human trafficking also includes the story of "M," an indigenous eighteen-year-old woman who was promised a job as a domestic worker with a salary of seventy-five dollars a week. Upon arriving at the place where she would work, she was informed that she would not receive her salary for two months because she had to cover the transportation costs. Later, she was told that she would have to work an additional twenty months without pay to compensate for accidentally breaking a decorative piece. "E" was pregnant and worked over twelve hours a day without basic freedoms.

Human trafficking also includes the story of Karola...a story she bravely shares with us so we can understand what human trafficking can look like and so we can continue to grow and learn about this atrocious crime to prevent it. To read her story, although difficult, is a blessing, considering that only 2 percent of human trafficking victims survive.[4]

---

4   "Sólo El 2% de Las Víctimas de Trata de Personas Logra Ser Rescatado." Diario Primera Edición, September 26, 2021. https://www.primeraedicion.com.ar/nota/100502166/solo-el-2-de-las-victimas-de-trata-de-personas-logra-ser-rescatado/.

We can try to categorize, describe, detail, and communicate in order to raise awareness about this crime, which objectifies human beings and uses them as commodities. However, to eradicate it, education and small actions are what needs to be done. Actions that are our responsibility as a society, actions infused with empathy and devoid of prejudice, extending a helping hand to those who need it. These actions can be as small as opening up dialogue and as significant as establishing shelters for survivors. Whether small or large, they are the responsibility of each and every one of us who have the freedom to speak up for those who don't.

CHAPTER 3:
1996

While the Spice Girls had their first number 1 hit, "Wannabe," Jerry Maguire was out in movie theaters, the American Pathfinder launched on its 310-million-mile mission to Mars, Nintendo released their newest gaming system N64, Princess Diana and Prince Charles got officially divorced, and Tickle Me Elmo was in every store, Karola's journey through the unimaginable had begun. She was just a kid, having turned thirteen in October of '95, who could have never even begun to imagine what was in store for her.

Karola is from Puebla, a city in Mexico renowned for its well-preserved colonial architecture, characterized by colorful facades, ornate churches, and historical buildings. The city's historic center is a UNESCO World Heritage site and features exquisite examples of Spanish colonial design with rich history and culture. It is a beautiful place, hub for traditional Mexican pottery (particularly the intricate Talavera ceramics we all love), extraordinary cuisine, prestigious universities and educational institutions, and even has a volcano, La Malinche, located about an hour and a half from the city.

Of course, I am generalizing, yet people from Puebla are known for their warm and friendly demeanor, always welcoming and hospitable. Like much of Mexican culture, family is central to their lives, where traditions, relationships, and gatherings are of great importance. There is a strong sense of unity and support within families, as well as a strong religious presence. Curiously enough, the history of Puebla includes periods of challenges and adversity, such as conflicts and battles. People from Puebla are often seen as resilient and determined, able to overcome challenges with a positive attitude.

Karola's family was a shining example of unity, love, and unwavering support. Her parents' love story is the foundation upon which their family is built, and they are not just partners in marriage; they are each other's best friends and confidantes. Their mutual respect and affection set the tone for the entire family. Their daughters added vitality, energy, and joy to every corner of their household. Each daughter with a unique personality, talents, and dreams, yet bound by an unbreakable sisterly bond. They support one another in everything they have ever done, and the values instilled by their parents continue to flourish to this day. Karola remembers how they would gather around the dining table every Sunday after church for a hearty homemade meal, savoring the chance to connect and share stories from their week.

Karola's parents had an active role in their daughters' lives while they were growing up, nurturing their passions and offering guidance submerged in kindness. In this close-knit family, love is abundant, laughter is cherished, and challenges are faced together. They serve as an inspiration to all who witness their genuine affection, unbreakable bond, and commitment to nurturing a strong, loving, and supportive family unit in spite of everything they went through.

At school, Karola was usually at the back of the line because of her height, got good grades, had many good friends, and was liked by her peers. She was a smart, creative, kind teen who had immense love and attention from her parents. She loved to read, particularly Sherlock Holmes, and practiced figure skating. She was cared for, loved, protected, and taken care of...she had an extraordinary life.

The chapters of her story that involved human trafficking began in a way she would have never, in her wildest nightmares, imagined. At the time, two of her three older sisters were part of an "academy," or music training program, that appeared to be promising in leading young women to stardom, where they were supposedly learning to sing, dance, and play different instruments. This "academy" was "led" by a man we will call Antonio (like Antonio Lopez de Santa Anna), an accomplished Mexican musician, producer, and manager to different Latin pop stars, referred to as King Midas by some, his success and creative genius was something that characterized him in the music industry. At the time, he managed a Mexican woman we will call Laura (like the singer Laura Branigan), in an extremely successful music career, as well as many other young women, many of them underage. In 1996, Antonio was forty-one years old, and Laura was twenty-eight. Many times, Laura and Antonio delegated certain tasks, some having to do with surveillance of the victims, to a woman we will call Jane (like Calamity Jane). Jane was married to Antonio when she was fifteen years old, had a brief and unfruitful musical career, and then got divorced. She continued to live with Antonio and Laura until the year 2000. Jane was twenty-six years old in 1996.

This "academy" worked based on supposed scholarships. Parents did not have to pay to enroll their children, *nor* were they paid to do so. Only if you were lucky enough to be selected through castings or would submit pictures and information that was posted in a magazine, were you able to participate. You could be interested in dancing or singing or simply being part of something that Laura was involved in.

Laura's magazines, famous in the '90s, had different "articles." They also had drawings done by Laura and supposed diary entries that she shared with her fans. Some copies had gossip and information about her "sexy" calendars. They were sold in newspaper stands all over Mexico and were also sold in the United States. She was *that* famous. It was another way to recruit "backup dancers," "backup singers," or young girls who wanted to be part of her entourage. I do not know for a fact if she was the one who wrote the part of the recruitment. What I do know is the magazines have her name, her picture, her drawings, as well as her supposed diary entries. The covers and some of the pages of these magazines can still be found online. A particular one I found says,

> Friend! This is the opportunity you've been waiting for! Yes! *Laura invites you to be one of her backup singers. If you have the following requirements: you are a super lover of music, have a good voice, have a good presence, have aptitudes for dance and have availability to travel, then we offer you: a good salary, excellent work environment, and the opportunity to have a future career as a solo artist.

Before I continue with the story, I must remind you to keep in mind that everything was different because it was the '90s. It was a time when people who wanted a music or television career did not have the option to upload videos that could become viral. Auditions and castings were different, and the awareness and information we have today are not even close to what we had once upon a time. It was a simpler time in some aspects, in others, just as scary as it is today.

Something else I would like to bring up, dear readers, is that no matter what judgmental thoughts might come to mind, we must remember that it is not our place to judge others. For those of us who are parents, we know that our children's well-being is our top-most priority, that we

29

always do the best we can to the best of our knowledge, and that kind people believe in the best in others. Karola and I have had many conversations about her parents, about how they began supporting two of their oldest daughters in the pursuit of their dreams of dance and music at the prestigious "academy" they had joined. They believed that their talent and dedication were recognized, and therefore, they were granted scholarships that allowed them to have a real shot at success. Karola's parents were proud and supportive, understanding the sacrifices required for their daughters to excel, continuing their family dynamic rooted in trust and a belief in the goodness of people. Just like the parents of anyone who wins a scholarship to study anything else, there was absolutely no way Karola's parents could know it was all a farce.

They signed contracts and had legal guidance to make sure their daughters were studying while in the "academy." They did not—ever—receive any money or pay a fee to have their daughters enroll in this "academy," and to the best of their knowledge, their daughters were learning from the very best and were given the best opportunity to achieve their dreams. They are no different from any other parents. From parents who send their children overseas to have the best opportunities, from parents who invest their heart, selflessly, in their children's sports, medical, or music careers. Every single child star we have seen throughout time has had parents who give everything they have and more to make that happen. Of course, there are situations we have seen when parents later on in life take advantage of their child's fame, but that is another story altogether. Karola's parents, as the parents of every other young girl who was part of this group at some point (it is said that throughout the years, it was about forty girls), fell into the trap.

Again, I remind you that when Karola's parents began their journey with Antonio and Laura with their oldest daughter, it was the early '90s. No internet, no GPS, no texting, no sending one's location. It was a time of landlines, letters, and printed pictures. There would be no possible way for them to suspect what was going on beneath the surface. Their daughters were in the hands of some of the most famous people in Mexico, so of course, they would be developing their artistic skills; what else could they be doing? They thought they had given them the best opportunity they could have.

In this image, Karola is pictured together with her sisters and Jane in the early '90s. Karola is showing an autograph from Laura.

As you can clearly see from the image, Karola was a child when her sisters were already part of this nightmare. What their parents would come to know years later was a shocking revelation that would shatter their sense of security. Their youngest daughter, Karola, had followed in her sisters' footsteps, unaware of the dark secret that was hidden in plain sight. As the truth came to light, the family faced a painful reckoning. The safe haven they had believed in had been compromised, and their daughters had been subjected to unthinkable experiences. The shock and heartbreak were palpable, and they dealt, for many years, with feelings of guilt and disbelief. How could they have not seen the signs? How could their trust have been so misplaced?

In the face of such atrocities, Karola's family rebuilt their foundation together, drawing on the strength of their bond and the values that had always guided them. The journey toward healing has been a difficult one, and as the years have gone by, the family's strength has become a testament to the power of love, unity, and their unbreakable bonds.

I mention judgment because many times, we think that we would do better. That we know more, that we would have done things differently...

and parting from a place of judgment does not allow us to learn; it makes us arrogant and, at the end of the day, ignorant. When our starting point is from a place of empathy and compassion, and, ideally, a place of grace, we can understand what others have experienced from a humane point of view and understand that this could happen to any of us. So, we open our hearts and our minds and learn from the experiences of others, which is one of the objectives of Karola telling her story.

Did you know that today, jobs are advertised by scammers the same way honest employers do? They do it online (in ads, on job sites, and on social media), in newspapers, and sometimes on TV and radio. They promise you a job when what they want is your personal information and/or your money.[5] Did you know that teens and college students seeking employment during the holiday season may be ensnared by criminals offering fake employment, potential education opportunities, and other scams through social media? Criminals—today—are using fake websites or post advertisements on legitimate employment portals and social networking websites to lure young people into illegal activities.[6]

After this brief interruption, let's get back to the story.

At the beginning of 1996, Karola was invited to Mexico City to audition for a soap opera for a particular role where she would supposedly be playing the younger version of one of her sisters. Since the beginning, there had been grooming. Karola remembers her interactions and conversations with Laura revolving around being told to act naturally, do anything Antonio asked her to do, and that her sisters' jobs would be impacted if she didn't get the part. All of this was in the sweetest, kindest tone of voice, in a loving, caring manner, by a famous, charismatic pop star. Can you imagine? She was told how beautiful and talented she was and how she could have an extraordinary career. She also recalls how, on several occasions, she was told things like that if she didn't get the part, she would just be one more mediocre small-town girl who didn't make it. It was all part of the manipulation, grooming, and coercion that took

---

5   "Job Scams." Federal Trade Commission Consumer Advice, n.d. https://consumer.ftc.gov/articles/job-scams.

6   Wilkins, Gale. "Teens Seeking Seasonal Employment, Beware Human Trafficking Scams." WRAL News, December 5, 2022. https://www.wral.com/story/teens-seeking-seasonal-employment-beware-human-trafficking-scams/20614153/.

place by these people constantly. It involved compliments followed by doubt, followed by support, followed by pressure.

From the beginning, the love Karola and her sisters had for each other would be used against them without them even being able to communicate with each other. In this "academy," there was a lot of drama among the victims brought upon by the victimizers. It was like being in middle school and having the teachers lead the teenage drama.

At a certain point, Karola had a conflict that was induced by lies told by the women who were at the head of the operation, particularly Laura. It was a conflict of competition for the alleged part. She was told not to share the conflict with anyone, and when Karola did so with one of her sisters, everyone found out. She remembers it like it was yesterday, how she was told by Laura how Antonio was extremely upset about this and that Karola had to apologize, or for sure, she would not get the part.

Drama is, without a doubt, part of life. Teenage drama, let's not go there. Yet this was not exactly a teenage drama; this was a drama created by adults to manipulate minors into doing what they wanted.

Karola ended up apologizing to Antonio, expressing to him that she really wanted the part (she was so worried about the repercussions her sisters would have if she didn't get it), and so, after a little time went by, Antonio forgave her and told her she had gotten the part (spoiler alert... the part didn't even exist).

For the part, she would need to be away from home for about a year. Her parents obviously didn't like the idea; she was barely in middle school, yet they were coerced into thinking it would all be all right, that Karola would continue learning with a private teacher, as their older daughters had, and would have the amazing opportunity to be in this soap opera. Antonio and Laura traveled to Puebla to discuss the terms of the contract with her parents, which stipulated Karola would always be with her sisters and studying when she wasn't working or taking part in the learning activities of the "academy." The reality is that Karola "studied" until eighth grade—they hired a teacher to do the work for her so that her parents would see the certificates and not suspect a thing.

The conversation that was had assured Karola's parents that she wouldn't take part in anything deemed indecent (like being pictured for a calendar with little clothes on) and that she would be paid 200 pesos a week (which back then was around twenty-six dollars) when she got the part. Karola was groomed and manipulated since the beginning and wanted her sisters to continue having opportunities. Her parents, with legal advice and a trustful heart, gave Karola the green light to be part of the "academy." And then, the nightmare officially began.

After the contract was signed, they went to Cuernavaca, a vibrant city located in the state of Morelos, Mexico, known for its pleasant climate, rich history, and beautiful surroundings. Its nickname is "the City of Eternal Spring" due to its beautiful year-round temperate weather. It is a weekend getaway for many who live in Mexico City, where Antonio owned a house.

As soon as Karola got there, she was looking for her sisters, yet they were nowhere to be found, and that is when she started noticing irregularities. Laura would spend a lot of time with Karola, craftily capitalizing on playing on sympathy to manipulate her. She would fabricate dramatic tales full of sorrow, personal hardship, and despair that tug at the heartstrings of a thirteen-year-old girl. Through tearful conversations and false vulnerabilities, Laura would intentionally evoke empathy from Karola, seemingly baring her soul, all the while calculatingly manipulating her emotions to orchestrate the outcomes.

Both her fame and her feigned vulnerability granted her unparalleled influence over many young women. She artfully crafted so many stories, drawing those around her further into her web of deceit. She exploited Karola's genuine kindness, using it as a weapon. As they grew "closer," Laura would give Karola "tips" (we have to remember that Laura was a very popular and successful pop star, spending time with a thirteen-year-old), who would also tell her that they were good people who didn't smoke, drink alcohol, or do drugs, and Karola believed her. Who wouldn't at that age? Karola also remembers how she would tell her something along the lines of "Just act naturally. Don't be shy or worry about anything," saying the human body is natural and normal and that private parts are just parts of the body. Laura and Jane would talk to Karola about topics that would make her extremely uncomfortable, specifically topics regarding sex.

They would talk about how sexual intercourse was normal, even at Karola's age, and that other girls in the group would have sex with Antonio because they were open-minded and brave enough to experience different things. The conversations would always include things like that Antonio was a good person who had gotten his heart broken and had suffered a lot, was extremely sensitive, and was a wonderful man, yet not a boy (obviously, he was forty-one!). All men cheated on their partners and caused them pain, but Antonio was different because he was open about it; he would have sex with different girls because that was natural male behavior, but he was open so as not to harm anyone's feelings. She said that Karola would have to have intercourse with other men to get her dream anyway because that is how things worked, and at least she knew how good of a man Antonio was. That this was a wonderful way to be, that he was extremely considerate, that it was so important to Laura for Antonio to be happy, and that any girl would be lucky to be in a relationship with him, trying to induce Karola into having feelings for him.

Karola would tell them she didn't feel comfortable talking about sexual intercourse, and Laura would say things like that was just a tabu because she was brought up to think sex was wrong, but that it is the most natural thing in the world, that her "morality" was that of a small-town girl, not an open-minded person. Mind you, of course, sex is not wrong, and with the right person, it can be the most wonderful thing in the world. A thirteen-year-old with a forty-one-year-old? That is absolutely wrong in every single possible way.

Karola would then say that it was not that she thought it was wrong but that it didn't interest her at all, to which the conversation turned into her being told that she should think about her sisters and how terrible it would be if she left, what that would mean for her sisters, and worse, for Antonio, who would be devastated because if she didn't agree, she would have to leave.

Laura would ask Karola questions that revolved around how she felt towards Antonio, to which she would answer that she cared for him only as a friend. The conversations would then turn even more uncomfortable for Karola, as she was told to tell him (that she cared for him) because it would make him extremely happy. Karola reiterated that she didn't want to give Antonio the wrong idea, yet was told to tell him anyway...and what happened next still makes Karola's stomach turn.

She remembers how, as this conversation was happening, Laura pulled her to his bedroom door, knocked, and ran away, leaving Karola there. When we were discussing this, Karola mentioned how she remembers completely freezing at that point, not knowing what to do, and feeling extremely stupid to be there and not say anything, so she said the following, "Laura told me to tell you that I care for you." To which he responded by hugging her tight and telling her something along the lines of being extremely happy to hear that. When Karola headed back to her room, she saw Laura waiting for her in the hallway, letting her know how happy she was and how important this was for Antonio.

When we got to this point of her story in one of our long conversations, Karola closed her eyes and took a deep breath. She then continued to recall how a couple of days after that incident, Antonio went to get her out of bed at about 3 a.m. in his underwear and took her to the living room to ask her to be his girlfriend. He told her that by being his girlfriend, she would have to have intercourse with him, yet before she could say anything, he kissed her. Karola was repulsed, half asleep, and did not understand what was going on, yet she didn't say anything because she was scared and had been groomed consistently and constantly prior to that moment. He then told her that to be his girlfriend, she would have to pass the tests he would give her; she accepted without knowing what they would be, which would come shortly after that day. We will not be discussing these "tests" in this book. All I can say is that there is no way to put into words what happened... although some words might begin to explain, like humiliation, exploitation, dehumanizing experiences, dignity shattering, and horrifying.

After that, he took her to his room.

He took off his clothes, got on top of her, and raped her. A twenty-eight-year-old woman groomed, coerced, and manipulated a thirteen-year-old girl to end up in a forty-one-year-old man's bedroom to get raped.

Karola remembers leaving the room in tears, shaking, unable to understand what had just happened. She hardly slept, and later on that morning, Laura approached her and started talking to her, telling her things like how she was glad Karola had cared for Antonio, that she had saved him, and that now that she was his girlfriend, she should know that his feelings for her were pure and true, but that nobody could know about it because nobody would understand.

What happened afterward, and for years, was worse. But among all of the atrocities that would become part of Karola's everyday life was that Laura would instruct her to completely undress in front of her and would then dress her up in lingerie on certain occasions before Antonio would rape her.

Towards the end of 1996, they went to Zihuatanejo, where Karola had her first experience of forced labor. At the beach, she and other girls had to do a lot of yard work with their bare hands, where there were lots of weeds and red ants, and they couldn't drink any water unless it was given to them. They weren't allowed to go to the bathroom and were under surveillance all the time, and Karola was just so frightened because she knew that if she didn't do what she was supposed to, her sisters would get beaten or raped. That's how they would manipulate, threaten, and abuse them; each one of the three sisters was held hostage so that the other two would do whatever it was they were told to do.

She recalls a particular day when she was punished because Antonio decided she had lied to him about something, and when he forgave her, she didn't have to do the yard work anymore but was beaten with a belt and then raped.

Please think of someone you know who is thirteen years old. If you don't know anyone that age, think of yourself at that age. Imagine what it was or would have been like to be away from your parents, but with the peace of mind that you were at least with your siblings. Think about the hope you might have had to make a dream come true, for your talents to be discovered, to believe you have a once-in-a-lifetime opportunity.

All right, now that we have our empathy in check, let's continue. As the weeks went by and Karola was alienated, Laura continued grooming her, trying to become her friend, and telling her that Antonio had cancer, was extremely depressed, and that Karola reminded him of his one true love. Karola remembers how these conversations involved tears, melodrama, manipulation, and everything we can think of to generate a desired effect. There were fourteen years of difference between Karola and Laura.... At that time, Laura was more than twice her age. She took her time, she tried to gain her trust, and she did everything a predator does to later destroy her prey.

During one of my conversations with Karola, when she opened up about this part of her story, she kept repeating how disgusted she felt. How she didn't understand absolutely anything that was going on, how she had never in her life imagined this would happen. She couldn't talk to anyone about this; she was physically hurt, repulsed, emotionally alienated, and terrified...so she had taken to writing in her diary. I love writing (obviously) and consider it an extraordinary tool when being unable to express our emotions verbally, yet for Karola, even writing would cause trouble. Like in every horror story, Laura found Karola's diary and showed it to Antonio, who later told Karola that when he read what she had written, it broke his heart. Believe it or not, this made her feel extremely guilty...severe manipulation can do that to a person.

Some weeks later, Karola told them she wanted to leave the group, and remembers Laura's reaction, warning her that if she did, her sisters' careers would be over. What happened was beyond her scariest nightmare. Antonio beat her with an electric cord on her back, legs, and behind. They locked her away in a room by herself, where she was not allowed to leave or speak to anybody. The only times she was allowed to leave the room was when she would go with Laura to different events.

After a particular social event, Antonio was very upset with all of the girls and had them enter his room, one by one, to brutally beat them with cables. He warned them that while he beat them, they couldn't make a sound, or the beating would be worse.

Each day that went by was worse than the one before. She was isolated and deprived, mostly locked inside the four walls of a room with no furniture. She couldn't understand what was happening, where her sisters were, what this was all about. Her access to basic necessities like food had been severely restricted, and as days turned into weeks and weeks into months, the toll of Karola's isolation and deprivation began to manifest in profound ways.

Her emotional journey through this nightmare grew increasingly harrowing; the persistent hunger and physical pain and discomfort made it difficult for her to listen to her own thoughts, and as her emotional and physical health deteriorated, she began to question her own self-worth, possessed by feelings of shame and inadequacy, getting caught in a cycle of despair. Each day felt like a struggle against the most overwhelming tide of negativity.

Her once-bright eyes lost their sparkle, and her smile, once radiant, disappeared. The walls that confined her seemed to close in, amplifying the silence that enveloped her existence. Karola's spirit, once vibrant and full of promise, started to fracture.

Karola pictured in 1995.

"Trust the LORD with all your heart, and do not lean on your own understanding. In all your ways acknowledge him, and he will make straight your paths" (Proverbs 3:5–6, ESV).

CHAPTER 4:
Grooming

Many people have never heard the term grooming. Sometimes, I wish I hadn't, either. Honestly, even if the truth will set us free, sometimes I do think that ignorance is bliss. Yet unfortunately, ignorance won't get us anywhere, so it is our responsibility to learn about all of these different things to be able to prevent both ourselves and our loved ones from falling into this trap.

Grooming can happen to anybody. Age, gender, race, sexual preference, and socioeconomic status don't make a difference. Grooming, my dear readers, can also happen to parents. Parents who adore their children and want nothing but the best for them. We have to remember, when it comes to everything that encompasses human trafficking, nobody is exempt—even if we think we are. This is why it is so important to understand this, to know that we are not, ever, completely safe. Knowing what grooming is and how it can happen to any and all of us is one of the first steps for preventing it. When we delve deep into our different experiences, I am sure we can recognize moments where we have experienced some type of grooming. Perhaps by people we thought knew more than we did, or maybe by people we admire profoundly. It has nothing to do with how smart we are. Many times, in my opinion, it has to do with being good people who would not do that to others; therefore, we don't even consider someone doing it to us.

Grooming is about someone building a relationship, emotional connection, and trust with someone else with the purpose of manipulating, exploiting, or abusing the other person. Just as this can happen to anyone, anyone can be a groomer. Sadly, even people we would never think capable of such a thing. It can happen over a short period or long period of time; it could be weeks or even years. Sometimes, groomers build relationships with the person's family or friends to gain their trust.

There are different types of grooming, which can be online, in person, or both. Grooming can be done by a stranger or someone we know and trust, even (take a deep breath) by a family member.

In online grooming, groomers tend to lie about who they are and send pictures of other people pretending to be them. Sometimes, it will

41

be younger people, close to the age of the person they are grooming. They might target one child at a time or contact lots of children very quickly and wait for responses. They coerce the victims to agree to the abuse and reduce the risk of being caught.

The relationship a groomer may build can take different forms:

- A romantic relationship.
- A mentor.
- An authority figure.
- A dominant and persistent figure.

Groomers can use the same sites, applications, and games as children and young people and spend time learning about the interests of whoever they are grooming, using the information to build a relationship. This can occur through:

- Social media networks.
- Text messages and messaging apps, like WhatsApp.
- Email.
- Text, voice, and video chats in forums.
- Games and apps.

Whether it be online or in person, groomers may use tactics like:

- Pretending to be younger.
- Giving advice or showing understanding.
- Buying gifts.
- Giving attention.
- Asking them on trips, outings, or holidays.

Groomers might also try and succeed in isolating their victims from their friends and family, making them feel dependent on them and giving the groomer power and control over them. They might use blackmail to make a person feel guilt and shame or introduce the idea of "secrets" to control, frighten, and intimidate. We have to remember that people who have unfortunately experienced grooming don't understand this is what is happening. Complicated feelings, including loyalty, love, admiration, fear, shame, distress, and confusion, are part of what makes everything so confusing.

In Karola's story, the grooming was done 360 degrees, for it involved her parents, her sisters, and herself...by people in a position of power. Karola's parents thought their daughters were in the best hands, and Karola ended up normalizing what she experienced because of the manipulation and coercion that preceded the grooming. Of course, we think we might understand it from the outside, yet from the inside, everything was extremely confusing.

It can be difficult to tell if a child is being groomed—the signs aren't always obvious and may be hidden. Older children might behave in a way that seems to be "normal" teenage behavior, masking underlying problems. Among many other reasons, this is why we have to have difficult and uncomfortable conversations with our loved ones and open and cultivate our communication. Even if a person who is experiencing grooming might feel extreme shame, if they know they can come to us and we will listen, be supportive, and again, not be judgmental, then that might be what helps them through.

Some of the signs you might see include:

- Being very secretive about how they're spending their time, including when online.
- Having an older boyfriend or girlfriend.
- Having money or new things like clothes and mobile phones that they can't or won't explain.
- Underage drinking or drug-taking.
- Spending more or less time online or on their devices.
- Being upset, withdrawn, or distressed.
- Sexualized behavior.
- Language or an understanding of sex that's not appropriate for their age.
- Spending more time away from home or going missing for periods of time.[7]

---

7   "Grooming." NSPCC, n.d. https://www.nspcc.org.uk/what-is-child-abuse/types-of-abuse/grooming/.

Although grooming can look differently depending on the case, it usually follows a similar pattern:

- Victim selection: The abusers observe possible victims and tend to select them based on accessibility or perceived vulnerability.

- Gaining access and isolating the victim: Abusers will try to separate a victim (physically and/or emotionally) from those protecting them and often seek out positions in which they have contact with minors.

- Trust development and keeping secrets: Abusers will attempt to gain the trust of a potential victim through gifts, attention, sharing "secrets," and other means to manipulate them into thinking they have a caring relationship and to guide them to keep the relationship secret.

- Desensitization to touch and discussion of sexual topics: Abusers will often start to touch a victim in ways that appear harmless, such as hugging, wrestling, and tickling, and later escalate to increasingly more sexual contact, such as massages or showering together. Abusers may also show the victim pornography or discuss sexual topics with them to introduce the idea of sexual contact.

Abusers will always attempt to make their behavior seem natural; they are often kind, helpful, and charming with the purpose of creating a trustworthy image and relationship with the victim, their family, and even the community.[8] It is extremely scary because we could all be vulnerable at any given time, and it is difficult to live in constant fear. That is why we need the information. We need to have difficult conversations with our loved ones, and we always have to stay alert. Fortunately, there are very many resources that can help us stay informed, a couple are: InternetMatters.org and the National Center for Missing and Exploited Children.[9]

These are difficult topics. I know, for a fact, that as a mother, there are times when I really don't want to learn about this. Yet, as parents, we must. We have to find out (yes, sometimes our children will lie to us) what social media platforms they have. Are they always accompanied

---

8   "Grooming: Know the Warning Signs." RAINN, July 10, 2020. https://www.rainn.org/news/grooming-know-warning-signs.
9   "Sextortion." National Center for Missing & Exploited Children, n.d. https://www.missingkids.org/theissues/sextortion.

while using them? That is practically impossible. Do we know for sure how they are emotionally? If they feel lonely, if they suffer from bullying, or if a stranger writes them nice things? We don't. Don't hate me for this, dear readers; do some research. Do your children want to be famous on TikTok? Mine do...and it scares me, but it's a reality. It is our role, our responsibility, to stay informed and remove the blindfolds from our eyes. We have to know what certain things mean, like: sexting, grooming, "packs," deep web. No matter how many restrictions we impose, how many parental controls we have at home, and how careful we are, times have changed. Strangers no longer offer us a lollipop in the park; most of them are hiding behind a screen, pretending to be children, waiting for the perfect moment to act. I know it's overwhelming, and that's why sometimes we choose to look the other way...but that has led us precisely to where we are today.

If our children talk to us about grooming, it is important to listen carefully to what they are saying, let them know they have done the right thing by telling us, tell them it's not their fault, say we take them seriously, not confront the alleged abuser, explain what we will do next, and report what they have told us as soon as possible.[10]

The FBI most often sees crimes against children begin when an adult:[11]

- Forges a relationship with a young victim online and then later arranges to meet and abuse the child.

- Coerces a child into producing sexually explicit images or videos through manipulation, gifts, or threats—a crime called sextortion. Sextortion begins when a predator reaches out to a young person over a game, app, or social media account. Through deception, manipulation, money, gifts, or threats, the predator convinces the young person to produce an explicit video or image. When the young person starts to resist requests to make more images, the criminal will use threats of harm or exposure of the early images to pressure the child to continue producing content.[12]

---

10   "Grooming." NSPCC, n.d. https://www.nspcc.org.uk/what-is-child-abuse/types-of-abuse/grooming/.
11   "Parents, Caregivers, Teachers: Protecting Your Kids." FBI, n.d. https://www.fbi.gov/how-we-can-help-you/parents-and-caregivers-protecting-your-kids.
12   "Stop Sextortion." FBI, September 3, 2019. https://www.fbi.gov/news/stories/stop-sextortion-youth-face-risk-online-090319.

According to the FBI, the most important advice for parents is to have open and ongoing conversations about safe and appropriate online behavior. Other advice to consider:[13]

- Educate yourself about the websites, software, games, and apps that your children use.

- Check their social media and gaming profiles and posts. Have conversations about what is appropriate to say or share.

- Explain to your kids that once images or comments are posted online, they can be shared with anyone and never truly disappear.

- Make sure your kids use privacy settings to restrict access to their online profiles.

- Tell your children to be extremely wary when communicating with anyone online whom they do not know in real life.

- Encourage kids to choose appropriate screen names and to create strong passwords.

- Make it a rule with your kids that they can't arrange to meet up with someone they met online without your knowledge and supervision.

- Stress to your children that making any kind of online threat, even if they think it's a joke, is a crime.

- Report any inappropriate contact between an adult and your child to law enforcement immediately. Notify the site they were using, too.

There is a Safe Online Surfing Program by the FBI that teaches students in grades three to eight how to navigate the web safely. It has age-appropriate lessons and games that cover topics like cyberbullying, protecting personal information, recognizing trustworthy and untrustworthy sites, and avoiding malware. This program is available both in English and Spanish, and anyone can complete the activities on the FBI SOS website, yet the testing and competition are only open to students in grades three to eight whose teachers have registered their public, private, or home schools through the SOS website: https://sos.fbi.gov/en/.

---

13   "Parents, Caregivers, Teachers: Protecting Your Kids." FBI, n.d. https://www.fbi.gov/how-we-can-help-you/parents-and-caregivers-protecting-your-kids.

To learn more about how to be safe online, I leave you the link to OnGuardOnline.

OnGuardOnline is overseen by the Federal Trade Commission in collaboration with various federal agencies. It operates in conjunction with the Stop Think Connect campaign, spearheaded by the Department of Homeland Security, and is a component of the National Initiative for Cybersecurity Education, led by the National Institute of Standards and Technology. This educational website serves as a valuable resource for educators, parents, children, and the general public, offering essential information on online safety: http://www.onguardonline.com.

CHAPTER 5:
Exposure

We are exposed, no matter how we see it. When I think back to the impact certain things had on my generation, I can fully understand why we experience certain things in certain ways. Without a doubt, I am one of those people who have an issue with the Disney I experienced as a child. Sometimes, it still makes me a little mad, particularly the part of what we consume without realizing it, that shapes who we are and our perspectives. Karola and I have discussed this with respect to our particular generation. We grew up watching and listening to ideas that revolved around believing men were the ones who "saved" women and not that "salvation" is mutual. It upsets me that what was deemed important, and what, according to these stories, validated us as women, was for a man to "find" us (because, of course, we are lost), "save" us (because we don't know how to solve our own problems), "love" us (because that's what matters, that another person, even an unknown prince, loves us, not that we know our worth and love ourselves), and thus, eternally grateful, we would live in a state of indebtedness that constantly fed our self-esteem, which, like a bottomless barrel, was at rock bottom.

If we think about it, even if it sounds a bit dramatic, everything we are exposed to contributes to how we think. And Disney, back then, communicated certain ideas that became part of our thought patterns. Let's take two minutes of our time and think about how everything we had at our disposal, in terms of "children's entertainment," reinforced these sexist ideas:

- Ariel had to stop being herself to fit into Prince Eric's world.
- Belle fell in love with her captor—Stockholm syndrome.
- Cinderella spent two hours with the prince, and simply because she danced well, spoke for two minutes, and had some chemistry, she got married as soon as he saved her from her stepmother.
- Aurora, don't even get me started on that whole kissing-while-unconscious thing...I don't even know how to structure it semantically without going off like a rollercoaster. But I'll leave you with the task of researching the original story of Sleeping

Beauty from the seventeenth century, where not only is she kissed while unconscious, but she is also raped, impregnated, and gives birth to the king's children while still unconscious.

Yes, sometimes, I get fixated on the topic; I'll give you that much. But what catches my attention is how, among all of us, we follow what is considered normal at the time, without even questioning it. So, returning to Disney, the princesses and sexism, what does make me think is how when we watched those princess stories, we truly believed in them and didn't pay more attention to the real-life princesses exploited in the media. The one who, due to the stress she was living, developed bulimia, depression, and constantly swam against the current of the status quo, and ended up losing her life in a tragic way.

Today, social media has taken the wheel, and it frightens me to know that the algorithms are more in tune with us than, sometimes, we are with ourselves. I read an article that said that TikTok's recommendation algorithm pushes self-harm and eating disorder content to teenagers within minutes of them expressing interest in the topics.[14] Honestly, why?

Apparently, when it comes to social media, the concept of integrity often finds itself overshadowed by other, more flamboyant forces. Within this bustling digital world, where information flows like a cascading stream (and sometimes, more like a tsunami), values like honesty, authenticity, and moral soundness can sometimes appear to be elusive fireflies in the night. Beyond the concept of integrity, there are other values that are, in turn, both influenced and reshaped by the dynamic forces at play in the digital arena. Social media platforms make money; that is their objective, not looking after people's well-being. Although, of course, each and every one of them has its upside, we must remember the platforms also expose users to the dark underbelly of cyberbullying and emotional desensitization, also casting shadows of self-doubt, as we constantly grapple with unending comparison, societal expectations, and are in a never-ending pursuit for the picture-perfect image.

Let's take thirty seconds to actually give some thought to the concept of privacy...in this day and age, we have none. I don't think we fully understand this, yet it is the world we live in and are part of, and therefore, we

---

14   Milmo, Dan, and Alex Hern. "TikTok Self-Harm Study Results 'Every Parent's Nightmare.'" The Guardian, December 15, 2022. https://amp.theguardian.com/technology/2022/dec/15/tiktok-self-harm-study-results-every-parents-nightmare.

have normalized so many things because we are experiencing boiling frog syndrome. Although sharing personal moments and anecdotes creates the feeling of an intimate virtual bond, the distinct line between public and private has been blurred in many ways, leaving us exposed. If this happens to us as adults, imagine what it is like for teenagers.

There is a reason why the stream of information that shows up on our accounts is called our feed. It feeds our brains with whatever we have chosen, both consciously and unconsciously, that we are interested in. The algorithms do the selections for us, and many times, without noticing, we end up feeding ourselves the same ideas over and over again until we believe they are the ultimate truth.

If we actually think about it, all of this is extremely confusing, and how can it not be? The World Wide Web became available to the broader public thirty years ago, in April 1993, and since then, it has grown and evolved faster than most of us can keep up with. I view social media as a hectic marketplace where marketing and sales find their digital stage, advertising brands, trends, ways of life, and, of course, individuals. All the filters and perfect selfies set the stage for a fantasy world none of us mortals can live up to. Yet, in the clamor to sell and self-promote, the limelight on ethical standards and transparent motivations becomes dim, creating a potential abyss where integrity is nowhere to be found.

The platforms themselves, and all of us in the digital journey, have a critical role to play that will set the tone for the future. We have to consciously plant seeds of critical thinking and fact-checking to cultivate a space for well-rounded, accurate content to flourish. Simultaneously, we have to be careful of what we and our children are exposed to. Everything we have such easy access to without even noticing impacts how we view ourselves, how we view life, and what we view as normal. Human trafficking online has grown exponentially. Through technology and the use of social media, buying and selling human beings has become as simple as a "click" on a keyboard.

On certain websites, men, women, and children were available for "purchase" with sexual acts as their "product" to sell, making it easier than ever for traffickers to find victims, even making forms of payment nearly untraceable. This is wildly concerning because there is no way to track those who are paying, therefore making it even more difficult for law enforcement to charge these criminals. Traffickers are able to "friend" and "follow" potential victims through various apps and begin the grooming process, to then be forced or manipulated into prostitution or lured with false promises of a job.[15]

Unfortunately, the number of boys and girls among the victims of trafficking has tripled in the last fifteen years, and the percentage of boys has multiplied by five, according to a new report published by the United Nations Office on Drugs and Crime (UNODC). According to the Global Report on Trafficking in Persons, girls are primarily trafficked for sexual exploitation, while boys are used for forced labor. In 2018, 148 countries detected and reported around 50,000 victims of human trafficking. However, given the hidden nature of this crime, the actual number of victims is much higher.[16]

The report shows that traffickers prey on the most vulnerable, such as migrants and unemployed individuals, and the recession induced by COVID-19 is likely to have put more people at risk.

The UNODC Executive Director Ghada Waly, in a statement, said,

> Millions of women, children, and men around the world are jobless, out of school, and without social support in the ongoing COVID-19 crisis, leaving them at greater risk of human trafficking. We need specific actions to prevent criminal traffickers from exploiting the pandemic to exploit the vulnerable.

She added that the report, along with the technical assistance provided by UNODC through its global programs and field network, aims to gather governments' responses to trafficking, end impunity, and support victims as part of integrated efforts to move forward from the pandemic.[17]

Women and girls continue to be the primary targets of human trafficking. Out of every ten victims detected worldwide in 2018, approximately five were adult women, and two were girls. Around 20 percent of the victims were adult men, and 15 percent were young boys. In the past fifteen

---

15   "Human Trafficking and the Internet." The Child Advocacy Center of Lapeer County, n.d. https://caclapeer.org/human-trafficking-the-internet/.
16   "Se Triplica El Número de Niños y Niñas Entre Las Víctimas de Trata de Personas A Nivel Mundial." United Nations, February 2, 2021. https://news.un.org/es/story/2021/02/1487422.
17   Ídem.

years, the number of victims has increased, and their profile has changed. The proportion of adult women decreased from over 70 percent to less than 50 percent in 2018, while the proportion of children has increased from around 10 percent to over 30 percent. During the same period, the proportion of adult men has nearly doubled, from around 10 percent to 20 percent in 2018. Overall, 5 percent of the victims were subjected to trafficking for sexual exploitation, 38 percent were exploited for forced labor, 6 percent were subjected to forced criminal activities, 1 percent were forced into begging, and a smaller number were subjected to forced marriages, organ extraction, and other purposes.[18]

The proportion of detected victims who have been trafficked for forced labor has steadily increased for over a decade. Victims are exploited in a wide range of economic sectors, particularly those where work is carried out in isolated circumstances, such as agriculture, construction, fishing, mining, and domestic work. The report details that globally, the majority of people prosecuted and convicted for this crime are still men, accounting for around 64 percent and 62 percent, respectively. Offenders can be members of organized crime groups, who traffic the vast majority of victims, individuals operating on their own, or small opportunistic groups.[19]

Traffickers see their victims as commodities, disregarding their dignity and human rights: they sell other human beings for prices ranging from tens of US dollars to tens of thousands, and large criminal organizations generate the highest profits. The investigation also points out that traffickers have integrated technology into their business model at every stage of the process, from recruitment to the exploitation of their victims. Traffickers approach many children on social media platforms, who can be easy targets in their search for acceptance, attention, or friendship. The organization has identified two types of strategies: "hunting," which involves a trafficker actively pursuing a victim, typically on social media, and "fishing," where perpetrators post job advertisements and wait for potential victims to respond. Furthermore, the internet enables traffickers to livestream the exploitation of their victims, allowing simultaneous abuse of a victim by many consumers worldwide.[20]

---

18   Ídem.
19   Ídem.
20   Ídem.

With data collected from 148 countries, UNODC was able to record 534 different trafficking flows worldwide, although victims are often trafficked within geographically close areas. A typical example is girls recruited from a suburban area and exploited in nearby motels or bars. Globally, the majority of victims are rescued in their country of origin.[21] Yet, terrifyingly and sadly enough, even within our own homes, abuse, manipulation, and even trafficking can take place. So can pornography.

As I mentioned in my book *La Estrella de Luna*, when I was a young teenager, there used to be Playboy magazines that my classmates would steal from their dads.[22] These magazines, which most men bought, and not "for the articles," featured naked women but in a somewhat artistic way. Maybe it was partly for the articles, I don't know, but the magazine had a Braille version since 1970, and this didn't include photographs, so let's say they had something more than just naked women.

You could see the women's breasts and their genitals. They posed artistically, considered it an achievement to appear in the magazine, and were acclaimed worldwide. It was a form of "art" to showcase the female body in all its splendor...with their consent. In 2016, the magazine decided to stop featuring completely naked women because they realized they couldn't compete with the freely available pornography on the internet. Nowadays, they have returned to featuring nudes.

Obviously, Playboy wasn't the only magazine that existed. There were others that showed very explicit photographs of sexual acts and women in less artistic poses. Of course, there were also pornographic films, clandestine theaters that showed these movies, or sex shops where you would go into a little room to watch pornography. It's not that it didn't exist before; it has always been around. What has changed with pornography nowadays is that it's free, widely accepted, and just a click away.

For better or for worse, at least before, there was some effort made by the customers to hide. Nowadays, there is increasingly more pornography, greater variety, easier access, and fewer consequences, so it has been normalized. How can something be so "normal," be free, and within our reach if it is harmful? Welcome to the twenty-first century.

The pornography to which everyone (including our children,

---

21   Ídem.
22   Caspi, Raquel. *La Estrella de Luna*. Ediquip, 2021.

regardless of their age) has free access to is cruel, objectifies women, and normalizes sexual violence. Before, the porn industry was also quite a spectacle; it had awards and everything.... With or without judgment, this industry took care of its actors and actresses, conducted tests for sexually transmitted diseases and HIV, put effort into the scenes, and often even into the plot. It was a multi-million-dollar industry that has now disappeared, and it disappeared because of the current pornography. Mainstream pornography is created by men who use women to please other men. All they need to make a video is a camera (which can be a cell phone) and a woman. There is so much—so much—competition, aside from the fact that most of it is free; the content that gets the most clicks is the most violent and abnormal. In mainstream pornography, women are penetrated, subjugated, degraded, demeaned, and objectified. Many times, they appear to be unconscious.

This eroticization of violence has a very strong impact on the mind of the viewer, as they learn to find it exciting in a way. Pornography affects the development of healthy sexuality, including understanding consensual sexual relationships and true pleasure. So now, misogynistic, disgusting, and subjugating pornography that objectifies women has become the primary sexual educator for teenagers, teaching them that engaging in violent fantasies is acceptable, regardless of their partner's opinion. It tends to repeat the same story: one or many men satisfy their sexual desires with a woman's body in a violent manner without considering what she may be feeling physically or emotionally. This "sexual education" is teaching us (both men and women) to sexualize female pain, disregard a woman's desires, and dominate her, turning sex into an obligation.

We know that this is not right because we know it. Knowing that this is happening and considered "normal" opens the door for us, in some way, to accept that just as marijuana is a gateway to other drugs (let's not argue, it is what it is), mainstream pornography is a gateway to other types of pornography, including child pornography.

Child pornography images are not protected by the First Amendment and are considered illegal under federal law. The United States Code, Title 18, Section 2256, defines child pornography as any visual representation involving a minor (someone under eighteen years old) engaged in sexually explicit conduct. This includes photos, videos, digitally created images resembling real minors, and images that seem to depict actual identifiable minors, even if altered or modified. It's important to note that sexually explicit conduct doesn't require images showing the child in sexual activity. Even a naked picture of a child can be considered illegal child pornography if it has suggestive qualities. The age of consent for sexual activity in a state is irrelevant; any depiction of a minor under eighteen engaged in sexually explicit conduct is against the law. Federal law prohibits the production, distribution, reception, and possession of child pornography through any means that involve interstate or foreign commerce. For instance, Section 2251 makes it illegal to coerce, induce, or persuade a minor into engaging in sexually explicit conduct for the purpose of creating visual depictions of such acts. Those who attempt or conspire to commit child pornography offenses are also liable for prosecution under federal law (see 18 U. S. C. § 2251; 18 U. S. C. § 2252; 18 U. S. C. § 2252A).[23]

Did you catch that it is illegal to possess child pornography? This is important to communicate to our loved ones. Even without the intention of doing anything wrong, and just by being "part of the gang," if anyone receives a picture of a minor that is suggestive in sexual nature and keeps it (or, in any case, forgets to delete it), it is against the law. We have to have difficult conversations and let our children know what all of this is about. We also have to explain that although they might be the ones thinking of sending pictures at a certain point, there is no guarantee they won't go viral and that they will be exposed. Times have changed, and we have to speak their language.

On the bright side, there are laws to protect us.

"Nonconsensual pornography" is when an image that is sexually graphic is shared without your consent, also known as "revenge porn." It is illegal to share or publicize intimate images without your consent, and it is against both civil and criminal law. These images can include:

- Images taken during the course of an intimate relationship (including images you took of yourself and shared with the intent to keep them private).

---

23   "Citizen's Guide to U.S. Federal Law on Child Pornography." Criminal Division, n.d. https://www.justice.gov/criminal/criminal-ceos/citizens-guide-us-federal-law-child-pornography#:~:text=Specifically%20percent2C%20percent20Section%20percent202251%20percent20makes%20percent20it,to%20percent20prosecution%20percent20under%20percent20federal%20percent20law.

- Hidden recordings.
- Images stolen from electronic devices (phones, computers, tablets, etc.).
- Recordings of sexual assaults.

Washington law states that it is a crime for a person age eighteen or older to knowingly disclose an intimate image of you when:

- The image was obtained under circumstances in which a reasonable person would know or understand that the image was to remain private.
- The person knows or should have known that you did not consent to the disclosure.
- The person knows or reasonably should know that disclosure would harm you.

In the criminal case, the first time someone is convicted of nonconsensual pornography, it is considered a gross misdemeanor. If the person does it again, it will be a felony charge, punishable by up to five years in prison and up to $10,000 in fines. In some situations, the person can also be charged with voyeurism in the first degree, which is also a felony. If you are under eighteen, depending on the circumstances, the perpetrator may also be charged with crimes related to child pornography.[24]

In a civil case, examples include claims of emotional distress, invasion of privacy, recovery for economic damages, lost earnings, and attorney's fees. The perpetrator could be ordered to pay for the emotional and economic damages. How much money that is will depend on the facts of your case. The court can also order the perpetrator to stop, which can be a helpful order to have.[25]

It is important to also know that if sexually explicit images of you are shared or publicized without your consent, it is a crime, even if you were the one who took the picture or video. You can file reports of nonconsensual pornography and/or voyeurism by calling or visiting the office of the police or sheriff where the crime occurred. The case will be investigated

24   "Know Your Rights: Non-Consensual Pornography ('Revenge Porn')." Legal Voice, August 2022. https://legalvoice.org/nonconsensual-pornography/.
25   Ídem.

and, if it is found that a crime was indeed committed, referred to the county prosecutor. It is considered advisable to work with a lawyer, due to the fact that it can be hard to know for sure where the perpetrator was when (s)he shared the image.[26]

Remember that undocumented immigrants are supposed to get the same help from law enforcement and the legal system as citizens and documented immigrants. However, it is advisable to first work with a lawyer or an advocate on a safety plan, including whether or not it is a good idea to contact law enforcement in your area.[27]

Although most internet platforms (social media, search engines, etc.) do not allow sexually explicit images to be posted, it is important to contact the platforms where the images have been posted and report the images for violating the terms of service. Remember to take screenshots of all images as they appear on all platforms as evidence for your case before contacting the companies. You can also hire a service to remove the images and monitor for any additional images. Some services offer discounts to victims of revenge porn and will offer free services for underage victims.[28]

So, I'm sure all of this information has been overwhelming. My suggestion, for now, is to take a deep breath, close your eyes, say a prayer, and be grateful. Gratitude is associated with many mental and physical benefits, and studies have shown that feeling thankful can improve sleep, immunity, and mood. It can also decrease anxiety, depression, difficulties with chronic pain, and risk of disease.

We have so much to be thankful for every day, and although, at times, living in this world may make our hearts a little heavy, just the possibility of having access to all of this information to be as proactive as we can is something to be thankful for.

Although there are now laws to protect us, and this is without a doubt a step in the right direction, there is still so much more to be done. One thing I consider extremely important to continue to propel this issue in the right direction is education. At home or at school, education plays a crucial role in the prevention of these crimes. We have to be brave enough

---

26   Ídem.
27   Ídem.
28   Idem.

to have these important yet difficult conversations to protect our loved ones and to continue to address how we can further learn and understand ways to help victims heal.

CHAPTER 6:
1997

While some of us might have been listening to Daft Punk, Fleetwood Mac, or Radiohead, pondering if Rose could have actually shared the raft and saved Jack in *Titanic*, the world was experiencing situations that would change the course of the future. Princess Diana and Mother Theresa died, Madeleine Albright became the first female secretary of state, and stock markets crashed. Karola was about to experience several crashes that year that she would never forget.

That year, after a show on TV that Laura was on ended, the group had now officially moved to a beach in Mexico they called the white beach. There, under the sun's unrelenting gaze with barely any clothes on, Karola was instructed to sweep across the sand, weed, and scrub the outside furniture for hours on end. Her hands were calloused and weathered, her throat dry, her stomach empty, and her heart heavy.

Every day, as Karola worked incessantly under the burning sun, her gaze would meet the ocean's vast expanse that taunted her with its promise of comfort and release. The relentless rhythm of sweeping, scrubbing, and weeding offered no respite, no chance to relieve herself from the heat by submerging in the water. She was not allowed to go into the ocean, and the ocean itself, once a sanctuary of boundless potential, had become some kind of distant mirage, a reminder of the freedoms denied. As the hours turned into days and the days into weeks, the harsh reality of what was truly happening began to unfold. It was a reality devoid of access to basic human rights; she had become a slave.

Then, as if what she and the other victims were living wasn't enough torture, Karola was introduced to another form of punishment: "The Box." The Box consisted of a container where all of the decaying food was placed, things like onion peels, egg shells, rotting tomatoes, and anything that was left over. Antonio would many times add water to this disgusting mixture and then make Karola and the other victims eat from it. That was her only source of food. If, for any reason, she would throw up, she had to eat what she had thrown up with a spoon.

Later that same year, Antonio fled Mexico because another victim, who had been Antonio's wife when she was still a minor and had managed to leave, was about to publish a book detailing the crimes that were happening behind closed doors. He went to Spain and divided up the girls that were held captive, sending some of them home to talk to their parents, telling them that the book was just a ploy from Antonio's ex-wife, together with a television network, to get back at them for not signing a contract. The intention was to later reunite with all of the girls abroad. Karola was one of them and remembers this moment as if it were yesterday. She remembers how she was carefully instructed by Laura to tell her parents a book would be published full of lies, and that Karola had won a scholarship to go to Spain to study film. She was extremely threatened and instructed to tell her parents that if they didn't let her go, she would run away from home because this was her dream. Although Karola's parents weren't pleased with their daughters living abroad, they ended up letting their daughters go to continue following her dream.

More rules had been set into place. What Karola remembers is that they could not speak directly to anyone from the opposite sex, could not show affection to anyone of the opposite sex (including family members), could not make eye contact with anyone, and if any male would accidentally touch them, even in the most irrelevant way or by accident, they had to defend themselves and tell Antonio. They were all threatened, oppressed, coerced, and manipulated; they were terrified.

Karola traveled with one of her sisters to Madrid, where they met Antonio and Laura at a Holiday Inn. From that moment, she lost access to her passport, and as the first days on a new continent went by, she had her first punishment. The reason for this punishment was that Antonio found out that Karola had been alone in her house while her parents went out to the market and her sister went to Sunday mass (Karola only had Antonio's permission to leave her house with her parents). For this punishment, while they were staying at a hotel, she was beaten with the electric cord of an iron and then raped.

As the rest of the girls arrived in Spain, they moved to another hotel and then to a chalet in a town called San Agustin de Guadalix. At this point, Karola was only allowed to eat whatever was leftover twice a day, while at the same time was told that she brought Antonio good luck and that she would be an example for success in Spain. She began to feel extremely sick to her stomach and would throw up constantly, which she was prohibited from doing. As it happened with "The Box," every time she would throw up, they would force her to eat what she had thrown up with a spoon, although the reason she was throwing up was different: Karola was pregnant. She was fourteen years old.

Karola recalls how, in June of that year, on any given day, Antonio decided he wanted to get some of the girls drunk, bought a bottle of vodka, and made Karola and the other girls drink it. She threw up and was told by Laura she had to get an abortion and that the baby was probably dead anyway because of how much alcohol she had drank.

Karola and I have had several conversations about this painful, heart-wrenching incident. She has mentioned to me, on different occasions, how psychologically it was much easier to heal from forced labor. Although her body bears scars that remind her of the cruel torture she was subjected to so many years ago, it seems like it all occurred in another lifetime. On the other hand, the sexual abuse, as well as being forced to have an abortion, took very many years of extremely difficult and painful work that, although it allowed her to transform her pain, left scars in her core.

When they got back to Spain, she hadn't been able to process everything that had happened, leaving her feeling completely broken. What followed was nothing short of torture. Again, allowed only to wear very light clothing, sometimes not even underwear, during extreme weather, Karola had to perform forced labor in the very large estate they had moved into. She had to clean the estate as well as do heavy yard work for hours on end, and on top of that, she had to carry a colossal rock back and forth. Her muscles, strained and trembled, weak from the lack of nutrients, would fail her often. When she would drop the rock, she was punished with a severe beating. Hour after hour, she would put one foot in front of the other, her chest heaving with exertion, while her legs burned with every step she took, protesting against the ceaseless demand placed upon them. She could feel the heat radiating from the rock, a searing reminder of the unrelenting weight she had to carry, a weight that seemed to grow heavier by the second. Her hands, calloused and bruised, her fingers full of dry blood, seemed to want to quit as she grasped the rock's rough surface with a tenacity born of desperation.

As the hours stretched into eternity, a sense of weakness would envelop her, like a thick fog that would take over her senses. Her limbs felt heavy and unresponsive, as if they were made of lead. She would stumble, her steps faltering, and a surge of panic would course through her veins. Dropping the rock was not an option, for the consequences were even worse than this punishment. Her vision would blur, and she would fight against the waves of dizziness that threatened to consume her. The world seemed to spin nonstop, a cruel reminder of the extreme toll that slavery and forced labor had taken. Every fiber of her being screamed for release from the unending cycle of carrying this burden, yet each new day was the same as the last. These memories are engrained both in her core and her body.

I do not understand the sick mind of a person who enacts the role of Hades with Sisyphus, punishing another human being in this cruel, inhumane way. To this day, Karola has scars from the rock on her arms and legs. When strangers ask her about them, she tells them she fell while riding her scooter.

In the confined realm of this golden cage, the disparity grew larger every passing day. Stranded in the unending nightmare of slavery, neglect, and abuse, Karola found herself trapped in a cruel routine that denied her the most basic sustenance. The pangs of hunger gnawed incessantly at her insides while Antonio and Laura lounged comfortably, indulging life while forcing deprivation. The aroma of cooked meals that remained tragically out of her reach would float through the air, reminding her that nourishment and fulfillment were perpetually denied.

Antonio and Laura, seemingly oblivious to her plight, reveled in a world of leisure. Seated comfortably, they partook in the act of eating with an air of casual indifference, their conversations punctuated by the clinking of cutlery and the soft glow of the television screen they would watch for hours. While they savored the flavors of their meals and had noticeably gained weight, Karola wrestled with the gnawing emptiness within her, continuing to subsist from the scraps of leftovers and remnants of rotting food that were begrudgingly bestowed upon her in "The Box."

Her days continued in scarcity, including the lack of human interactions. The absence of conversation, the weight of her unspoken thoughts, emotions, and words bore down upon her like an invisible burden, as heavy as the rock she had to carry. The walls that enclosed her became both her sanctuary and her prison, a space where her voice echoed back to her in hollow reverberations, carving away at her sense of self.

She was able to see her sisters from time to time, one of them also being forced to work for hours on end, but they were not allowed to even look at each other. Their bodies were in the same space, but they were each suffering their own personal prison. The isolation robbed her of the mirror that others provided, reflecting back her thoughts and feelings, validating her existence, and making her feel human.

The emotional toll was palpable, and the isolation only exacerbated her insecurities, self-doubt, and rumination, leading her to question her worth, her place in the world, and whether her thoughts and feelings held any significance at all. The absence of a listening ear amplified the storms of emotion that raged within her. The sorrow, together with the frustration, anger, and hopelessness, left her trapped in an endless cycle of despair.

*Picture taken of Karola and her sisters
while in Spain to send to their parents.*

"Because you know that the testing of your faith produces perseverance" (James 1:3, NIV).

CHAPTER 7:
Forced Labor and Sex Trafficking

According to the State Department, the United States recognizes two primary forms of trafficking in persons: forced labor and sex trafficking.[29] To further understand human trafficking, we must know that the definition of this crime can be simplified by using a three-element framework focused on the trafficker's acts, means, and purpose.

Forced labor, also called labor trafficking, involves the extent of the activities involved when a person uses fraud, force, or coercion to exploit the labor or services of another person.

The "acts" element of forced labor is met when the trafficker recruits, harbors, transports, provides, or obtains a person for labor or services. The "means" element of forced labor includes a trafficker's use of fraud, force, or coercion. The coercive scheme can involve different things, such as threats of force, debt manipulation, withholding of pay, confiscation of identity documents, psychological coercion, reputational harm, manipulation of the use of addictive substances, threats to other people, or any other forms of coercion. The "purpose" element focuses on the perpetrator's goal to exploit a person's labor or services. Sadly, there is no limit on the location or type of industry because this crime can be committed in any setting or sector, including but not limited to agricultural fields, factories, restaurants, hotels, massage parlors, retail stores, fishing vessels, mines, private homes, or drug trafficking operations.[30]

All three elements are essential to constitute the crime of forced labor.

There are certain types of forced labor that are frequently distinguished for emphasis or because they are widespread:

DOMESTIC SERVITUDE

"Domestic servitude" is a form of forced labor in which the trafficker requires a victim to perform work in a private residence, creating circumstances of unique vulnerabilities. Domestic workers are often isolated

---

29   "Understanding Human Trafficking." U.S. Department of State, December 12, 2023. https://www.state.gov/what-is-trafficking-in-persons/.

30   Ídem.

and may work alone in a house while their employer might control their access to food, transportation, and housing.[31]

FORCED CHILD LABOR

The term "forced child labor" describes forced labor schemes in which traffickers pressure children to work. Traffickers often target children because they are more vulnerable. Although some children may legally engage in certain forms of work, forcing or coercing children to work remains illegal. Many forms of slavery or slavery-like practices—including the sale of children, forced or compulsory child labor, and debt bondage and serfdom of children—continue to exist despite legal prohibitions and widespread condemnation. Some indicators of forced child labor include situations in which the child appears to be in the custody of a non-family member, and the child's work financially benefits someone outside the child's family, or the denial of food, rest, or schooling to a child who is working.[32]

SEX TRAFFICKING

Sex trafficking envelops the range of activities involved when a trafficker uses force, fraud, or coercion to compel another person to engage in a commercial sex act or causes a child to engage in a commercial sex act.

The crime of sex trafficking is also understood through the "acts," "means," and "purpose" structure. All three elements are required to establish a sex trafficking crime (with the exception of child sex trafficking, where the means are irrelevant).

The "acts" element of sex trafficking is met when a trafficker recruits, harbors, transports, provides, obtains, patronizes, or solicits another person to engage in commercial sex.

The "means" element of sex trafficking occurs when a trafficker uses force, fraud, or coercion. Coercion in the case of sex trafficking includes the extensive array of means included in the forced labor definition. These can include threats of serious harm, psychological harm, reputational harm, threats to others, and debt manipulation. The "purpose" element is

---

31 Ídem.
32 Ídem.

a commercial sex act. Sex trafficking can take place in private homes, massage parlors, hotels, or brothels, among other locations, as well as online.[33]

CHILD SEX TRAFFICKING

In cases where an individual engages in any of the specified "acts" with a child (under the age of eighteen), the means element is irrelevant regardless of existent evidence of fraud, force, or coercion. The use of children in commercial sex is prohibited by law in the United States and most countries around the world.[34]

CONSENT

Human trafficking can take place even if the victim initially consented to provide labor, services, or commercial sex acts. The analysis is primarily focused on the trafficker's conduct and not that of the victim. A trafficker can target a victim after a victim applies for a job or migrates to earn a living. The trafficker's exploitative scheme is what matters, not a victim's prior consent or ability to meaningfully consent thereafter. Likewise, in a sex trafficking case, an adult victim's initial willingness to engage in commercial sex acts is not relevant, whereas a perpetrator subsequently uses force, fraud, or coercion to exploit the victim and cause them to continue engaging in the same acts. In the case of child sex trafficking, the consent of the victim is never relevant, as a child cannot legally consent to commercial sex.[35]

As you can see, dear readers, the complexity of what happened to Karola was surreal. Something we discussed in one of our conversations was the lack of information she had with respect to what exactly had happened to her. An unimaginable nightmare? Without a doubt. Yet when she started learning about human trafficking and was able to put a name to this nightmare, everything changed for her. That is what information can do for all of us. When we are able to label certain situations, we can emotionally begin to integrate our experiences. When, years later, she had the opportunity to do this, and to understand that what was done to her was also a crime, other things inside her began to fall into place

33   Ídem.
34   Ídem.
35   Ídem.

as well. Yet, although I personally believe that crimes deserve retributive justice, Karola often talks to me about divine justice, giving me the gift of expanding my heart while my head is pulling in the other direction.

CHAPTER 8:
Women Are Traffickers Too

Even though sex trafficking is seen traditionally as a male-perpetrated offense, female traffickers may be as common as male traffickers. Somehow, as a woman, it's a tough pill to swallow, but I figure it's better to know these things than to believe otherwise and be fooled by preconceived notions of how we believe things are; stereotypes are never helpful.

Oftentimes, female traffickers were victims themselves and were unfortunately and tragically exposed to the lifestyle early on. Abuse and trauma play important roles in their development, propelling them to transform from victim to victimizer. Almost fifteen years ago, the United Nations highlighted that "in some parts of the world, women trafficking women is the norm."[36]

There is danger in creating and continuing gender-based stereotypes. This allows female traffickers to continue to operate under the radar to the point of being almost invisible. Unfortunate cases like actress Allison Mack with DOS in NXIVM and Ghislaine Maxwell, who was found guilty of sex trafficking in connection with Jeffrey Epstein and sentenced to twenty years in prison, are current examples that unfortunately, yet fortunately, have come to our attention.[37]

According to researchers, other roles can include:

- Second-in-command to the head female or male trafficker.
- Often in charge of managing victims, securing or forging counterfeit legal documents, transporting victims, bribing law enforcement and business institutions, and overseeing sex-work operations.
- Responsible for cash handling, grooming new victims, sex-work internet advertising, and regular oversight of victims.

---

36   Sarrica, F., Jandl, M., Borneto, C., Korenblik, A., Brown, S., Kunnen, S., & Kuttnig, K. Global Report on TRAFFICKING IN PERSONS. Policy Analysis and Research Branch of UNODC, 2009.

37   Withers, Mellissa. "Sex Traffickers: The Hidden Role of Women." Psychology Today, March 13, 2023. https://www.psychologytoday.com/us/blog/modern-day-slavery/202303/sex-traffickers-the-hidden-role-of-women.

- Voluntary participation in sex trafficking due to relational ties (romantic, familial, or business) with male sex traffickers.
- Typically, women are responsible for the business side of sex trafficking, such as managing brothels, bath-houses, escort services, clubs, and other related establishments.[38]

Recent research and personal interviews reveal that many women become perpetrators because they have been victims of sex trafficking themselves, usually for the greater part of their lives. Furthermore, many women engaged in the commercial sex trade as traffickers, because they are forced to do this by their traffickers, might be promised they will no longer have to perform sex work if they can take on a different role within the organization.[39]

Other common motives for women to engage in sex trafficking voluntarily include:

- Early exposure to the sex industry.
- Early exposure to the sex trafficking industry.
- Parent/relative involvement with the commercial sex industry or trafficking.
- Parent/relative selling their children into the sex trafficking industry.
- Low socio-economic status families, forcing women to search for fast money at a young age.
- Close physical proximity to high trafficking involvement areas.
- Previous sex trafficking victims may be trying to earn their freedom or choosing to be perpetrators to avoid the trauma of being a victim.
- History of mental, physical, and sexual trauma in childhood.
- Lack of education and economic resources.

---

38   Veldhuizen-Ochodničanová, Eva, and Elizabeth L. Jeglic. "Of Madams, Mentors and Mistresses: Conceptualising the Female Sex Trafficker in the United States." ScienceDirect, March 2021. https://doi.org/10.1016/j.ijlcj.2020.100455.
39   Withers, Mellissa. "Sex Traffickers: The Hidden Role of Women." Psychology Today, March 13, 2023. https://www.psychologytoday.com/us/blog/modern-day-slavery/202303/sex-traffickers-the-hidden-role-of-women.

- Pimps often provide food, housing, and other necessities to female traffickers that work for them.

- Many women without proper education, stable income, special skills, or professional skills are cornered into trafficking to survive or provide for their families.

- Sense of belonging or family.

- Female traffickers can also be products of the foster care system or have no family contact.

- Victims who have been taken away from their families at a young age or have little contact with their families can have nowhere to turn for a safety net in tough times.[40]

Gateway occupations and activities can lead women down a path that leads to involvement in criminal activities. Both criminal and non-criminal occupations and activities can act as a catalyst for women to eventually become involved in sex trafficking. Examples of non-criminal professions that may lead to sex trafficking include stripping, OnlyFans, pornography, "sugar babies/daddies/mamas," child acting, and modeling.[41]

Although there is plenty of information that leads to the constant debate on what factors contribute to victims becoming victimizers, there are cases where victimizers make themselves out to be victims. It is extremely confusing and difficult to understand and discern. I found an article by Leslie Vernick LCSW I want to share with you, it has a couple of examples that help clarify this.[42]

When Victims become Villains and Victimizers Claim they are Victims

I've noticed a disturbing phenomenon that often happens when a victim of abuse speaks out and tells the truth about what's

---

40   Ídem.

41   Love, D. A., Fukushima, A. I., Rogers, T. N., Petersen, E., Brooks, E., & Rogers, C. R. Challenges to Reintegration: A Qualitative Intrinsic Case-Study of Convicted Female Sex Traffickers. Feminist Criminology, 2021. 155708512110450.

42   Vernick, Leslie. When victims become villains and victimizers claim they are victims, n.d. https://leslievernick.com/counselors/wp-content/uploads/2019/02/When-Victimizers-Cry-Victim.pdf.

going on at home. Or, when she asks for help, protection, and/ or justice from those who are mandated by God to protect her. In public cases, such as the recent Stanford University rape case or the mounting accusations against Bill Cosby for sexual abuse, what happens in the public eye is that the victim is repeatedly discredited, scrutinized, and eventually portrayed as the villain. We often hear things like, "She is lying" or "She is ruining his life, his career, or the family."

In the Stanford University rape case that was all over the news last year, the freshman swimming star Brock Allen Turner was found guilty of three counts of sexual assault. Yet his father wrote an impassioned letter to the court stating, "Brock's life is ruined, his swimming future forfeited for 20 minutes of action." Notice the twist of language. Brock has now become the victim. In his father's letter, Brock is portrayed as being inexperienced with alcohol and his behavior described as promiscuous rather than abusive. Sympathy was sought for the victimizer (reflected in the sentencing of only 6 months) and turned against the victim, portraying her as the villain who "ruined" his future. What about her future?

If you've paid attention to the unfolding story of Bill Cosby, I hope you've noticed a similar strategy. Initially, most people did not believe the women who accused Cosby of drugging and raping them, even though their stories were eerily similar. People said, "Surely these women were opportunists, looking for attention and money from one of America's most beloved icons." The female victims were painted as villains, their lives scrutinized, and Bill Cosby was the victim of their lies and money grabbing motives. Yet as more and more sordid details come to light, it looks like most people judged these women too harshly. One woman will have the opportunity to tell her story before a jury as Cosby is finally going to trial. And you can see these cases for yourself by googling them.[43]

I share these incidents because I often see the same thing happening with women who seek help from their church leaders for marital abuse. There is the sad and public story of Naghmed

---

43   http://www.cnn.com/2016/05/24/us/bill-cosbyhearing/

Abedini, who fiercely advocated for three years for her husband's release from an Iranian prison. She was Christianity's darling until she exposed that her hero husband, Saeed, had regularly abused her during their marriage.[44] Suddenly she was no longer Christianity's darling. She was not believed or supported by some prominent Christian leaders who had been very involved in her crusade to have her husband released. Now her words were questioned, her mental health and morality suspect. She became the villain and her spouse looked like the victim of an angry and/ or unstable spouse. I've seen this happen over and over again in my work with women in destructive marriages. Why is it so hard for us as Christian people helpers and leaders to believe her and so easy for us to dismiss her and make her the villain? I'd be curious to hear your opinions, but in my experience, there are three main reasons we do this.

1. Victims are imperfect and sinful. When we look at the Stanford University rape case, we see a woman who drank too much alcohol and left the party highly intoxicated. What was she thinking? Or we say to ourselves why would women go to Bill Cosby's home or be with him unless they were also mutually guilty of sexual sin. It's all too easy to look at the victim's flaws and failures, question her story, and believe those who subtly or boldly discredit her character. For those of us in the church, a female victim slides into the villain role, especially if she is angry, acts a little rough around the edges, or implements tough consequences such as separation, or divorce. She's told, "You are the problem here. You have a hard heart, you are unforgiving, you are ruining the family, you must be having an affair, you want to break up the home, you've been listening to worldly influences, you are ungodly, you're crazy, you're un-submissive, you're rebellious" – and on and on.

2. The second reason we find it so easy to misjudge what's really happening is because the one who is being accused of abuse, serial adultery, or other destructive patterns is very often a very charming and convincing liar. He may also hold a position of power in the church or community and no one could imagine

44   https://www.washingtonpost.com/news/acts-of-faith/wp/2016/02/01/the-strangecase-of-the-pastor-released-from-iran-and-his-wifes-abuse-allegations/

him guilty of the things his wife accuses him of. Or, if the evidence is irrefutable, he now becomes penitent, "sorry" for what he's done and that's supposed to make everything better. Church folks rally around the seemingly "repentant" one and he now becomes the victim of her hard heart and firm boundaries. He receives the church's love and support and she gets shunned and disciplined for not falling into line with what the church leaders think she should do. Even when she tells her church leadership that his innocence or repentance is bogus and his behaviors haven't changed, she is often vilified and discredited. She's told she's judgmental, hard-hearted and lacking grace. Somehow, they know him better than she does, even though she's lived with him for years.

3. The third reason is that we're uneducated on the dynamics of abusive behaviors and destructive relationships, and too proud or too busy to really dig deeper to see, over time, what's really going on. We're also afraid to do or say anything that would make it look like we are endorsing a marital separation or divorce, so it's just easier to tell the victim to be quiet, forbear, forgive and make the best of things. AND, when she refuses and gets louder, or more demanding for justice, she becomes the villain.

In the Bible, there is a horrific story of a victimizer turned victim and the leaders of Israel fell for his story without investigating what really happened. A Levite husband shoved his concubine wife out the door to an angry crowd to do as they pleased in order to save his own skin. Raped and beaten all night long, she crawled to the doorstep of the house in the early morning and died. The Levite callously tossed her broken and battered body on his donkey, took her home, and later cut her up into twelve pieces. He sent one piece to each of the twelve tribes of Israel, portraying himself (not his wife) as the victim of a horrible injustice (see Judges 19:1–30). And the scary and horrible thing is that they believed him. As Biblical counselors and well-meaning church leaders, let's not get duped.

Let's not forget that there are wolves in sheep's clothing that are excellent liars and do a very good job of pretending they are sheep, when in fact they are wolves. And there are imperfect and sinful people out there who are true victims that we need to believe and protect. I am so glad you are on this site. It shows me that you care about people who are true victims and want to help. Contact us to find out how you can be a better counselor or advocate for those who need our help.

I think we can understand clearly, after reading this, how things can seem very different from how they actually are. In the different examples, people with "power" change or modify their story, deny their responsibility, and revictimize the victim. This, too, has happened to Karola. It has also happened to her parents.

In the complex universe of human behavior, the enigma of why certain victims become victimizers while others defy that trajectory remains a perplexing puzzle with no definitive solution. It's a complicated interplay of psychology, circumstances, and a tug and pull of nature and nurture.

The research on this topic provides no definite answer, just a complex web of psychological dynamics. For some, the imprint of trauma, added to the residue of suffering, can influence the way they perceive themselves and the world around them. The pain they endured might fester into a toxic cycle, driving them to replicate their own anguish upon others. The transformation from victim to victimizer can be a defense mechanism, a desperate attempt to reclaim a sense of power in a world that once left them powerless.

For others, the trauma becomes a catalyst for transformation. It's through their pain that empathy and compassion are born. They choose a different route, one that seeks to break the chains of victimization and contribute to the healing of others, guided by a deep understanding of the darkness they've experienced.

Circumstances also play an important role in the equation. Support systems, resources, and opportunities for growth and healing shape the trajectory of the journey. Yet, without underplaying the importance of all the different factors, the role of personal agency, in my opinion, is at the top of the list. Even within the direct circumstances, the power of individual choice is what differentiates survivors from victimizers. Every single person has the opportunity to refuse to let experiences define us and to refuse to perpetuate a cycle of harm. Although we have all heard how "hurt people hurt people," hurt people have a choice. Karola harnessed her pain as a catalyst for change, channeling her energy into breaking the chains of victimhood and transforming her suffering into a force for good.

In the end, the question of why some victims become victimizers while others do not remains a very complex enigma where, among other factors, psychology, circumstance, resilience, and personal agency play a part.

CHAPTER 9:
1998

While some of us were rooting for France when they won the World Cup, appalled by the Bill Clinton-Monica Lewinsky scandal, enamored by Joseph Fiennes in Shakespeare in Love, and couldn't get that song from Chumbawamba out of our heads, Karola was entering her third year in the most unimaginable nightmare.

Still a victim of sexual abuse and forced labor, Karola was now threatened that if she didn't do as told, particularly with the heavy rock she had to carry as she walked back and forth, Antonio would beat a child that another victim had brought to life, who at the time was three-months-old. Exposed to extreme weather with barely any clothes, little access to food which wasn't really even food, and raped consistently, Karola couldn't understand why it was all happening.

She would have to bathe either outside while it rained or with "ecological baths," which consisted of waking up at dawn and being subjected to Antonio "rinsing" her with freezing water. This was apparently for her own good because it was healthy, and since they didn't "waste" any gas, it was good for ecological purposes. Of course, there were no towels to dry off, and at night, Karola would sleep on the cold floor with only a light bed sheet and no pillow. Her day would begin at around 7 a.m. and would end at about 2 a.m. She wasn't eating or sleeping enough. About halfway through the year, Antonio, Laura, and most of the girls moved to Argentina. There, towards the last quarter of that year, Karola became pregnant again.

It was prohibited to be close to the windows—some of them were even covered up—or to go to the door unless otherwise instructed by Antonio. If, for any reason, someone went to the house, the girls held captive would have to go and hide in a bedroom.

Even pregnant with his child, Antonio would continue to beat Karola relentlessly and obligate her to perform forced labor. In the nightmare of her captivity, she had no possessions, just the same old clothes she had to wear every day and a pair of white cotton tennis shoes. These shoes, though worn and tattered, carried with them a weight of symbolism that anchored her to a semblance of normalcy in an otherwise surreal existence. With them came the seemingly impossible task that defied all reason: the shoes had to be impeccably clean.

The very act of wearing white cotton tennis shoes in her grueling circumstances seemed exceedingly absurd. She wasn't even allowed to bathe properly and toiled in the dirt, mud, and filth, yet she was expected to maintain these shoes in a state of pristine purity. This demand was yet another testament to the sadistic nature of her captors, a reminder of her limited resources and the dehumanizing conditions to which she was subjected.

As the days stretched on, dirt embedded itself into the very fabric. Yet, despite the visible signs of wear, she clung to the task of keeping them clean as if her life depended on it. Because somehow, it did.

There is another particular moment engraved in Karola's memory. As she worked outside while rain fell incessantly, covering the landscape in a murky coat of rain and mud, she lost her balance, and one of the tennis shoes slipped from her foot. Contrary to Cinderella, this lost shoe would not be a piece of the puzzle of her happy ending but one more reason to be tortured.

The squelching mud seemed to swallow the shoe whole as a wave of panic gripped her heart when she heard Antonio's voice. His words, dripping with calculated cruelty, fell upon her like a death sentence. For every fifteen minutes without the recovery of her lost shoe, she would have to perform a full day of labor (twenty-four hours). The pressure of time, already a cruel currency, made the task even harder. As her mind was racing, her body slowed down by the extreme exhaustion. She fetched a shovel and thrust relentlessly into the earth as she gritted her teeth. Each second that went by reminded her of the impending consequences, a type of agonizing countdown for imminent torture.

Minutes blurred into hours of sweat-soaked effort and rising desperation. Every shovelful of mud had become automatic, and even though every muscle in her arms felt like it was on fire, she did not stop. Finally, she found the shoe that appeared to be swallowed by the earth, and the weight of those hours seemed to lift, only for a fleeting moment. As soon as she informed Antonio she had found the shoe, he proceeded to beat her relentlessly.

Her body, already weakened by the incessant demands of forced labor and perpetual abuse, now bore the additional weight of pregnancy, and although within a fragile vessel, a life took root, a tiny beacon of hope that seemed to defy the very brutality of its inception.

It was during the moment of scrubbing the white cotton tennis shoes clean, as tears cascaded down her cheeks, that a subtle shift occurred within her. Amidst the rhythmic motion of her hands, an instinctual impulse emerged that stirred from deep within her core—a whispered prayer, a desperate plea that flowed from her lips. A connection, imperceptible from the outside yet undeniably powerful, began to take root. It was as if the very act of scrubbing, of expending the little energy reserve she had, sparked a flicker of light. Her tears of despair transformed, becoming a baptism of sorts, cleansing her heart and suspending her, for a brief moment, in limbo between agony and hope.

This act of prayer offered a lifeline to a source of strength that seemed to defy the reality she was subjected to.

She remembers how a couple of days after this particular incident, she received another brutal beating as a punishment for another victim who could not perform the forced labor Antonio demanded due to the horrifying effects of malnutrition. So, he instructed Karola to take off her clothes in front of the other young woman and beat her with a horse whip.

Towards the end of the year, Antonio enforced a new routine for his victims, which included excessive physical exercise that lasted about eighteen hours a day with no breaks. Like with all the other tasks they were forced to do, the victims would supervise one another, knowing that they would have to tell on each other if something didn't go according to Antonio's plan, even if they didn't want to. These grueling exercise routines, combined with the anemia they had all developed, would leave the victims even more depleted, a reminder that even if they didn't have "work" to do, they would not be left alone.

With aching muscles and spirits dulled by the weight of their circumstances, the victims became purveyors of popsicles, their hands shaping frozen confections that offered a fleeting taste of sweetness amidst the bitter reality they faced. The streets, a realm of freedom and possibility for others, were a haunting stage where their innocence was bartered away for mere scraps of sustenance. Of course, the money they made was not theirs to spend.

In the midst of this agonizing existence, hygiene products, symbols of normalcy and self-respect, remained tantalizingly out of reach, a stark reminder that their captors reveled in stripping them of every fragment of their humanity. The absence of a toothbrush symbolized a profound neglect of their well-being. Toothpaste and shampoo? A distant luxury. Toilet paper, a fundamental element of human dignity, was beyond their reach, emphasizing the dehumanizing conditions to which they were subjected. Even the most elemental acts of self-care were rendered impossible.

The denial of these basic necessities was a calculated act of psychological manipulation, a means of exerting control by destroying their sense of self-worth. In denying them the basic tools of self-care, their captors sought to extinguish the flickers of individuality that remained. Adding insult to injury, they were prohibited from cutting their hair, reinforcing their powerlessness and reducing them to mere shells, stripped of their own identity.

On one particular occasion, as the weight of her suffering threatened to crush her spirit, she mustered the courage to talk to Antonio, daring to initiate a conversation that she knew was against the rules. She voiced her hope for a healthier pregnancy, wanting to give her baby a better chance to enter the world. It was a plea born out of maternal love and determination to protect her child. Her voice trembled as she articulated words full of hope that hung in the air. It was a plea for mercy, and despite the fact that Karola was carrying his child, Antonio's answer was one of pure cruelty.

He told her she could never leave and that if she tried, he would make her have an abortion, even if that meant putting a broken bottle inside her. At this moment, she was about four months pregnant. Her punishment for wanting to leave, apart from the exploitation that had been going on for years, consisted of being belted with the buckle fifty times a day. As the end of the year approached, and Christmas was around the corner, Antonio decided to "forgive her," and the beatings stopped for a small period of time. She spent an extremely traumatic Christmas in Argentina, and toward the last days of the year, they all left for Brazil.

During one of our conversations, Karola told me about her pregnancy; we talked about everything she went through and about what it is like to carry a child.

CHAPTER 9: 1998

The journey of motherhood is a profound chapter in the book of human experience. For those who bear life within their wombs, the phenomenon is ineffable, a voyage into the depths of existence that lacks the correct words to do it justice. Physiologically, cellular division, growth, and transformation is a miracle that unfolds with a precision that science can unravel. Emotionally, it is a journey of anticipation, vulnerability, courage, and every emotion in between. It is a transformation that unfolds from within and becomes a leap of faith. The journey of motherhood is one of transforming and becoming, of nurturing life from within.

In this journey of uncharted territory, Karola would pray constantly, asking God to protect her and her son.

"Say: 'What a lioness was your mother among the lions! She lay down among them and reared her cubs" (Ezekiel 19:2, NIV).

CHAPTER 10:
Mothers

As a child, I remember hearing a beautiful belief about the power of mothers' love. During the weekly Shabbat ritual, as the sun sets on Friday and ushers in a day of rest, mothers light candles and say a prayer for their families. It is said that at this moment, mothers can ask for anything they wish for their children, and their prayers will be answered. How incredible is that? The responsibility of this special moment lies with mothers, and through their loving devotion, they bring blessings to their families. Many women also include a special prayer, written by and for women, that reminds us of the strength and grace that comes from within.

In Judaism, Shabbat holds many meanings, but one could say that spiritually, it is the soul of the week, where the energy that invigorates the week and the culmination to which the effort is focused merge. On this day, the actions of the previous week reach their purpose and elevation, and in the same way, the plans for the next week are blessed.

It seems that when I was around nine years old, my curiosity about the "power of motherhood" began to grow. How was it possible for mothers to have the influence to care for their children through prayer? I asked my mom to make specific requests, and of course, when some of them were fulfilled, I attributed it to my mother's prayers. This was the moment when the seed of the magic that exists between a mother and her child was planted within me.

Years later, while I studied special education, during my third semester of practice, is when I had my first encounter with the experiences of various mothers and their children, especially those with language, learning, and hearing difficulties, as well as Down syndrome. Although I couldn't fully grasp what these mothers were going through, what struck me the most was their unwavering love, devotion, and commitment to helping their children succeed. Despite my young age and lack of personal knowledge about motherhood, I was in awe of these incredible mothers. I was amazed at how well they knew their children and how they could interpret their needs even when communication was a challenge. Every progress, no matter how small, was a major achievement for them. I was fortunate to develop close relationships with the mothers of the children I worked with, who taught me firsthand that the bond between a mother and child is indescribable. They were exceptional teachers, and I am grateful for the lessons they taught me.

As I began my professional journey during my last year of university, I had the privilege of working at a private clinic where I had even more encounters with various mothers who trusted me to work with their children. My admiration, respect, and fascination for these women and their relationships with their children continued to grow. However, I remember a particular progress report session, years after working there, for a child who presented significant difficulties and was a challenge for everyone involved.

While discussing the progress and areas of opportunity with the mother, she asked me, "Are you a mom?" to which I replied, no.

I remember her disapproving face and how, from that moment on, she directed her attention solely to my boss. I felt frustrated, upset, and undervalued. I didn't understand how years of professional experience, my work with her child, and my empathy towards them as a family were disregarded simply because I wasn't a mother myself. It wasn't until many years later that I fully comprehended the weight and significance of that moment.

Returning to my experience as a Jewish woman, it is customary to immerse oneself in the waters of the mikvah on the Shabbat before getting married. The mikvah is a natural body of water that must be filled with living waters from a source that flows continuously, such as spring water, rainwater, or even melted snow. The woman who leads this ritual explains that water is the primary source of all life and has the power to purify, restore, and replenish life. It is recommended to go to the mikvah when one undergoes a change in status, where life "nullifies death," and thus, the transition to a state of purity is completed.

Experiencing the mikvah is truly a profound and indescribable experience, and it's one that has a powerful impact on the women who participate in it. During the ritual, the woman who leads the ceremony imparts a special message to the mother of the bride, entrusting her to be with her daughter until the moment of her wedding. The leader explains that the physical and spiritual presence of the mother serves as a protective shield for her daughter, safeguarding her from any adverse situations that may affect her due to her heightened vulnerability and openness. The love of a mother envelops her daughter, and her intuition serves as a guiding force. It truly is a magical and inspiring moment.

Becoming a mother has been the most extraordinary experience in my personal life. It has also been so for Karola. Many times, she has told me that being pregnant with who we will call Jonathan (which means gift from God) saved her life, even if, at the time, her fear was overwhelming. You see, Antonio threatened his victims, telling them that the females that were born would eventually become his partners and that he would kill the males.

Several years ago, during an investigation I was doing while studying transpersonal psychology, I found an article that blew my mind: "Male Microchimerism in the Human Female Brain."[45] In this study, they quantified male DNA in the human female brain as a marker for micro-chimerism of fetal origin (i.e., acquisition of male DNA by a woman while bearing a male fetus).

Among all of their findings, they encountered that male Mc is frequent and widely distributed in the human female brain. As I read this study, what impacted me the most was realizing that our children, from the very inception of their existence, become a part of us as we become a part of them. We exchange sparks of our essence as we carry them within, cultivating a connection during the months of coexistence that transcends the tangible. This connection takes root in the very fibers of our being, defying the boundaries of space and time.

When I shared this study with Karola, we had one of the most moving conversations, as we agreed on the idea that the journey of motherhood, no matter what it might look like for each person, is not a solitary path or a physical connection that ends after giving birth, but a two-way connection that is boundless and eternal.

---

45   Chan, William F. N., Cécile Gurnot, Thomas J. Montine, Joshua A. Sonnen, Katherine A. Guthrie, and J. Lee Nelson. "Male Microchimerism in the Human Female Brain." PLOS ONE, September 26, 2012. https://journals.plos.org/plosone/article?id=10.1371%2Fjournal.pone.0045592.

CHAPTER 11:
Violence against Women

All mothers are women, and we are all here by the grace of God through our mothers, who were our vessels. We were all in our mother's wombs, so it is unfathomable to me how there is so much hatred against women. I remember when, a long time ago, I heard that in China, they killed babies if they were girls; it was truly something that I could not find space for in my mind and heart. When I was pregnant with my daughter, my parents next-door neighbor told me, "May God bless you with a boy in your next pregnancy." I kid you not.

Clearly, I hadn't understood that the machismo we are exposed to and that we normalize (both men and women) has taken us to the extreme we find ourselves in today. It seems like we've gone back to the Middle Ages. Every day—without exception, I see news of new missing women in Mexico. *Every day*. I am a woman, and I have a mother and friends who are part of 52 percent of the Mexican population. A population at risk of being murdered for being women. Gender violence is something that continues to shock me, even with everything I know about it. Yes, I understand that it has to do with harming a person or a group of people purely based on their gender. I understand that it is linked to inequality and the abuse of power. Of course, it is also inherently linked to human trafficking. But still, I can't understand it.

I don't understand how it is possible for this to be happening so strongly and frequently, but what I understand even less is that this reality is denied, rationalized, justified, and accepted. Femicides are the extreme manifestation of gender violence, and apparently, in Mexico, they happen every day. Gender violence only discriminates gender—social, environmental, cultural, economic, and educational contexts don't matter here.

The United Nations defines violence against women as,

> Any act of gender-based violence that results in, or is likely to result in, physical, sexual, or mental harm or suffering to women, including threats of such acts, coercion or arbitrary deprivation of liberty, whether occurring in public or in private life.[46]

---

46   United Nations. Declaration on the elimination of violence against women. New York : UN, 1993.

Intimate partner violence refers to behavior by an intimate partner or ex-partner that causes physical, sexual, or psychological harm, including physical aggression, sexual coercion, psychological abuse, and controlling behaviors.

Sexual violence is "any sexual act, attempt to obtain a sexual act, or other act directed against a person's sexuality using coercion, by any person regardless of their relationship to the victim, in any setting. It includes rape, defined as the physically forced or otherwise coerced penetration of the vulva or anus with a penis, other body part or object, attempted rape, unwanted sexual touching and other non-contact forms."[47]

According to the World Health Organization, here are some facts:

- Violence against women—particularly intimate partner violence and sexual violence—is a major public health problem and a violation of women's human rights.

- Estimates published by WHO indicate that globally, about one in three (30 percent) of women worldwide have been subjected to either physical and/or sexual intimate partner violence or non-partner sexual violence in their lifetime.

- Most of this violence is intimate partner violence. Worldwide, almost one-third (27 percent) of women aged between fifteen and forty-nine years old who have been in a relationship report that they have been subjected to some form of physical and/or sexual violence by their intimate partner.

- Violence can negatively affect women's physical, mental, sexual, and reproductive health and may increase the risk of acquiring HIV in some settings.

- Violence against women is preventable. The health sector has an important role to play in providing comprehensive health care to women subjected to violence and as an entry point for referring women to other support services they may need.[48]

Population-level surveys based on reports from survivors provide the most accurate estimates of the prevalence of intimate partner violence

---

47   "Violence against Women." World Health Organization, n.d. https://www.who.int/news-room/fact-sheets/detail/violence-against-women.
48   "Violence against Women." World Health Organization, n.d. https://www.who.int/news-room/fact-sheets/detail/violence-against-women.

and sexual violence. A 2018 analysis of prevalence data from 2000–2018 across 161 countries and areas, conducted by WHO on behalf of the UN Interagency working group on violence against women, found that worldwide, nearly one in three, or 30 percent, of women have been subjected to physical and/or sexual violence by an intimate partner or non-partner sexual violence or both.[49]

Over a quarter of women aged between fifteen and forty-nine years old who have been in a relationship have been subjected to physical and/or sexual violence by their intimate partner at least once in their lifetime (since age fifteen). The prevalence estimates of lifetime intimate partner violence range from 20 percent in the Western Pacific, 22 percent in high-income countries and Europe, and 25 percent in the WHO Regions of the Americas to 33 percent in the WHO African region, 31 percent in the WHO Eastern Mediterranean region, and 33 percent in the WHO South-East Asia region.[50]

Globally, as many as 38 percent of all murders of women are committed by intimate partners. In addition to intimate partner violence, globally, 6 percent of women report having been sexually assaulted by someone other than a partner, although data for non-partner sexual violence are more limited. Intimate partner and sexual violence are mostly perpetrated by men against women. Without a doubt, gender inequality and norms on the acceptability of violence against women are the root causes of violence against women.[51]

Intimate partner (physical, sexual, and psychological) and sexual violence cause serious short and long-term physical, mental, sexual, and reproductive health problems for women. They also affect their children's health and well-being. This violence leads to high social and economic costs for women, their families, and societies.[52] Such violence can:

---

49   Violence against women Prevalence Estimates, 2018. Global, regional and national prevalence estimates for intimate partner violence against women and global and regional prevalence estimates for non-partner sexual violence against women. WHO: Geneva, 2021.

50   "Violence against Women." World Health Organization, n.d. https://www.who.int/news-room/fact-sheets/detail/violence-against-women.

51   Ídem.

52   WHO, LSHTM, SAMRC. Global and regional estimates of violence against women: prevalence and health impacts of intimate partner violence and non-partner sexual violence. WHO: Geneva, 2013.

- Have fatal outcomes like homicide or suicide.

- Lead to injuries, with 42 percent of women who experience intimate partner violence reporting an injury as a consequence of this violence.

- Lead to unintended pregnancies, induced abortions, gynecological problems, and sexually transmitted infections, including HIV. WHO's 2013 study on the health burden associated with violence against women found that women who had been physically or sexually abused were one point five times more likely to have a sexually transmitted infection and, in some regions, HIV, compared to women who had not experienced partner violence. They are also twice as likely to have an abortion.

- Intimate partner violence in pregnancy also increases the likelihood of miscarriage, stillbirth, preterm delivery, and low birth weight babies. The same 2013 study showed that women who experienced intimate partner violence were 16 percent more likely to suffer a miscarriage and 41 percent more likely to have a preterm birth.

- These forms of violence can lead to depression, post-traumatic stress and other anxiety disorders, sleep difficulties, eating disorders, and suicide attempts. The 2013 analysis found that women who have experienced intimate partner violence were almost twice as likely to experience depression and drinking problems.

- Health effects can also include headaches, pain syndromes (back pain, abdominal pain, chronic pelvic pain), gastrointestinal disorders, limited mobility, and poor overall health.

- Sexual violence, particularly during childhood, can lead to increased smoking, substance use, and risky sexual behaviors. It is also associated with the perpetration of violence (for males) and being a victim of violence (for females).

Again, even if, while reading this, our hearts are heavy, there is an upside. There is growing evidence on what works to prevent violence against women, based on well-designed evaluations, and in 2019, WHO and UN Women, with endorsement from twelve other UN and bilateral agencies, published RESPECT Women—an extraordinary framework with the objective of preventing violence against women aimed at policymakers.

Each letter of RESPECT stands for one of seven strategies: Relationship skills strengthening; empowerment of women; services ensured; poverty reduced; enabling environments (schools, workplaces, public spaces) created; child and adolescent abuse prevented; and transformed attitudes, beliefs, and norms. For each of these seven strategies, there are a range of interventions in low- and high-resource settings with varying degrees of evidence of effectiveness. Examples of promising interventions include psychosocial support and psychological interventions for survivors of intimate partner violence, combined economic and social empowerment programs, cash transfers, working with couples to improve communication and relationship skills, community mobilization interventions to change unequal gender norms, school programs that enhance safety in schools and reduce/eliminate harsh punishment and include curricula that challenge gender stereotypes and promote relationships based on equality and consent, and group-based participatory education with women and men to generate critical reflections about unequal gender power relationships.[53]

RESPECT additionally emphasizes that effective measures are those that give precedence to the security of women, whose fundamental components entail questioning inequitable power dynamics between genders, encourage active participation, tackle various factors contributing to risk through integrated initiatives, and commence early in individuals' lifespan. In order to attain enduring transformation, it is crucial to enact and uphold laws, as well as devise and execute policies that foster gender parity, allocate resources for prevention and response, and allocate investments to organizations advocating for women's rights.[54]

Whilst averting and addressing violence directed at women necessitates a cross-cutting strategy, the healthcare sphere possesses a significant part to fulfill. The healthcare sphere can:

- Contribute to early identification and intervention by promptly recognizing signs of violence and providing appropriate support and care.

---

53   "Violence against Women." World Health Organization, n.d. https://www.who.int/news-room/fact-sheets/detail/violence-against-women.
54   "RESPECT Women – Preventing Violence against Women." World Health Organization, April 6, 2019. https://www.who.int/publications/i/item/WHO-RHR-18.19.

- Foster survivor-centered care by ensuring that the needs and preferences of survivors are respected and prioritized in the provision of services.

- Collaborate with other sectors, such as law enforcement, social services, and legal systems, to enhance coordination and information sharing for comprehensive support.

- Advocate for policy changes and allocate resources to enhance prevention, response, and survivor support.

- Train healthcare professionals on gender-based violence, its impact on health, and appropriate care practices.

- Engage in research and data collection to better understand the prevalence, causes, and consequences of violence against women and inform evidence-based interventions.

- Promote community awareness and education to challenge harmful gender norms, promote respectful relationships, and prevent violence against women.

By embracing these approaches, the healthcare sector can contribute significantly to the prevention and response efforts addressing violence against women.[55]

We can also make a difference! Here are some actions that we can take:

- Personal Education: Learn about the various forms of violence against women, its causes, and its impact on individuals and society. Stay informed about the signs of abuse and the available resources for support.

- Challenge Gender Stereotypes: Examine and question traditional gender roles and stereotypes that perpetuate inequality and contribute to violence. Encourage equality and respect in your personal relationships, and teach children and young people about healthy relationships based on mutual respect and consent.

- Speak Out: If you witness or hear about instances of violence or abusive behavior, speak up against it. Do not tolerate or remain silent about violence, and support survivors by believing and validating their experiences.

---

55   "Violence against Women." World Health Organization, n.d. https://www.who.int/news-room/fact-sheets/detail/violence-against-women.

- Support and Empower Survivors: Be a compassionate listener and provide support to survivors of violence. Encourage them to seek professional help, such as counseling or legal assistance, and respect their choices and decisions.

- Intervene Safely: If you witness a situation where someone is being harassed or abused, assess the risks and intervene if it is safe to do so. This can involve distracting the perpetrator, seeking help from authorities, or creating a safe space for the survivor.

- Promote Consent and Respect: Advocate for the importance of consent in all relationships and situations. Encourage open conversations about consent and respect, emphasizing the need for clear and enthusiastic consent in all interactions.

- Be an Ally: Support organizations and initiatives working to end violence against women. Volunteer your time, donate to relevant causes, or participate in awareness campaigns and events. Amplify the voices of survivors and activists fighting against gender-based violence.

- Educate Others: Share your knowledge and engage in conversations with friends, family, and colleagues about the issue of violence against women. Help raise awareness, challenge misconceptions, and promote a culture of respect and equality.

- Hold Perpetrators Accountable: If you encounter instances of abusive behavior or witness someone engaging in harmful actions, hold the perpetrators accountable by reporting it to the appropriate authorities. Encourage the implementation and enforcement of laws and policies that protect women's rights and ensure justice for survivors.

- Practice Self-Reflection: Continually assess your own attitudes, beliefs, and behaviors to ensure they align with respect, equality, and non-violence. Be willing to acknowledge and unlearn any harmful biases or actions that contribute to a culture of violence.

We must remember that preventing violence against women requires collective effort and sustained commitment. By taking these actions, we can contribute to creating a safer and more equitable society for all.

CHAPTER 12:
1999

While *Who Wants to Be a Millionaire* premiered on American television for the first time, we were downloading songs on Napster without understanding the ramifications, the euro was first introduced, *The Sixth Sense* shocked us all with its surprise ending, Bill Gates predicted the future of smartphones, and we couldn't listen to the radio without Cher's "Believe" or Britney Spears "Baby One More Time" coming on, "Wanted" posters circled around many parts of the world searching for Laura and Antonio.

In Pedra de Guarativa, Brazil, they were fugitives, but that didn't stop the torture. Since they now lived in raunchy hotels where they would not be recognized, they didn't want to draw any attention, so the punishments, although brutal, were quieter. Karola told me how she had to be in a room, sitting in the same position for hours without moving, and the only reason she was allowed to move was to exercise. She was still eating rotten food, and when she wasn't, she was given burnt chicken fat leftover from when Antonio and Laura would have roasted chicken. She felt she was in a zombie-like state while Antonio appeared to be angrier at her than at anyone else, and Karola thinks it had to do with the fact that she was pregnant with a boy.

She remembers how, on another occasion, Antonio called in one of Karola's sisters while she was in the room and asked her what she was thinking. For him, one of the worst offenses was to be lied to, so when she answered something trivial, he decided she was lying and started beating Karola. He kept beating her, threatening her sister that he would kill her if she continued lying. He would do this often with the different victims, torturing them both physically and psychologically for no apparent reason.

They were constantly on the move and arrived at an apartment building in Araruama, Brazil. There were three menus available.... The first one, for Antonio and Laura, which was rich in variety; the second one, for some of the victims who had been the role of helping them, like Jane; and the third, for victims like Karola and her sisters, which consisted of decomposing food, fruit and vegetable peels, and burnt chicken fat. Karola needed to go to the doctor since her pregnancy was very advanced, and she was instructed to find a cheap hospital to give birth at, where she would give a fake ID and could not give any information to anybody about anything.

She had to constantly tell Antonio, "Please, punish me," "I must remind you to punish me, please," "I'm sorry, please. However you want to fix things is good, please," and "I know I have done things wrong and I want to fix them, please, to be able to be with you." She was also instructed to go to Antonio's bedroom after he had had intercourse with another victim to tell him, "I want things to be right between us. Please, tell me what I need to do for everything to be alright between us."

The torture was constant. It was physical, sexual, psychological, and emotional...then on June 6th, 1999, who we will call Jonathan (name that means gift from God) was born.

Karola arrived at a public hospital in Brazil without having the opportunity to have a shower in over a month. She smelled terrible and was embarrassed, ashamed, and terrified. She was carefully instructed on what information to give and was threatened with the life of her child that if she gave anyone information about their whereabouts, she would never see her son again. From the first moment she saw her son, she knew something had shifted inside her; it was an instant connection she had never felt before.

Against all odds, Jonathan was born healthy, and as soon as they left the hospital, he was taken away from Karola. She was told she couldn't look at, hold, kiss, cuddle, speak to, or feed her son unless Antonio instructed otherwise. She could only see him when Antonio decided she could feed him and was instructed not to look at him or speak to him. She wasn't allowed to speak about her son to anyone either.

She was locked in a room and instructed to stay in the same position for hours on end, and you know what she would do? She would pray. Every once in a while, they brought Jonathan for her to feed him, and she would tell him, with her heart, how much she loved him and would pray to God for her son's protection. Then, someone would come in and take him away again. At that point, Karola had experienced so much excruciating pain that she was profoundly depressed, yet she continued to pray.

Two months after becoming a mother, she was back to being forced to exercise eighteen hours a day. She didn't have access to nutritional food and was not producing enough milk for her son. Jonathan was very skinny, but she knew she couldn't mention it to anyone, let alone Antonio. She feared that if she did, he would kill her son or give him away like they had done with another victim's son, so she would pray. She prayed to God for Jonathan's safety, for his health, for his future. She prayed to God for a miracle.

One afternoon, she was in the laundry room and noticed a window. If she would manage to go out the window (they were on the third floor), she could land on the balcony of the building next door and get help. She did. The neighbors were worried about her, probably because of the way she looked and the fact that she had clearly tried to escape. She became terrified, made up a story, wasn't thinking straight at all, and before she knew it, one of her sisters was ringing the neighbor's doorbell. When she saw her, she knew she was in trouble; she worried for Jonathan's safety, and she didn't quite understand why she had actually done that. Her sister handed her a cell phone, and Antonio was on the other end of the call. She told him she wanted to leave, she couldn't take it anymore, that she knew her son would be better off without her just because of the fact that keeping them away from each other gave Antonio so much pleasure; she knew they could never be together. Antonio was worried…he didn't want to alert anyone to their location, so he promised Karola over the phone that he would give her Jonathan and that she would be able to leave. She was also worried about her sisters; one of them had recently given birth to a baby girl, and she knew all of the horrible situations that could get worse if she didn't return, so she did.

Of course, Antonio didn't give Karola her son; he only beat her and locked her in a room. Several days went by, and when she was allowed to leave the room, she went to the kitchen down a hallway that had a window. Antonio asked her why she was a prostitute who liked people watching her with little clothes on and then continued insulting her and locking her back in the room. He later asked one of the others to bring Jonathan to him and, in front of Karola, started hitting the baby in the face. He was black and blue, and she knew she would never be able to escape with her baby. She knew he would do everything to torture them for as long as he lived, yet she continued praying.

"Therefore I tell you, whatever you ask in prayer, believe that you have received it, and it will be yours" (Mark 11:24, ESV).

CHAPTER 13:
Prayer

Although I am a spiritual person, I am also a scientist. From a very early age, I would ask my father non-stop questions about Judaism, annoying him to no end. I'm still that person. Yes, I pray. Yes, I believe in God. Yes, I like to investigate and corroborate my different hypotheses. That is just who I am. And as an ordinary human being, I also know that, in reality, we really don't know much. I don't mean to be discouraging, yet sometimes it feels to me that we, the human race, are maybe in a phase similar to the "terrible twos." But don't worry, dear readers; this chapter won't be about that!

I find spirituality extremely interesting, and as Karola and I have discussed several times, these are her words, "When I am connected to God, I feel my soul is in tune with the divine." I love this. I love it because, for those of us who have felt this connection and know how it can shift everything inside us and, therefore, around us, it really does feel this way.

There is an article, "The Science of Prayer," from The Wall Street Journal that explains how there is little research on any health benefits of prayer, mainly because of a lack of funding in the medical community for spiritual research.[56] Prayer is also difficult to study because, to be able to measure its impact, researchers need to find people who are open to praying but don't do it currently and who would be open to doing it.

A 2005 examination published in the Journal of Behavioral Medicine contrasting secular and spiritual modalities of meditation discovered that spiritual meditation induced a greater sense of serenity. In secular meditation, the focal point lies in directing attention towards aspects like breath or nonspiritual terms. Conversely, in spiritual meditation, the emphasis is placed on a spiritual word or text. Study participants were categorized into different groups, with some receiving instruction on meditating with self-affirming words ("I am love"), while others were taught to meditate using words that portrayed a divine entity ("God is love"). Subsequently, they engaged in twenty minutes of daily meditation for a duration of four weeks.[57]

---

56 "The Science of Prayer." Association for Psychological Science - APS, May 20, 2020. https://www.psychologicalscience.org/news/the-science-of-prayer-2.html.
57 Ídem.

Certain researchers in the field of prayer believe that individuals who engage in prayer derive benefits from experiencing emotional support. Consider the analogy of carrying a backpack throughout the hours. Gradually, it starts feeling overwhelmingly burdensome. However, if one can temporarily transfer the burden to someone else for a while, it feels lighter when resumed.

"This is akin to what prayer can achieve," explains Amy Wachholtz, an associate professor and director of clinical health psychology at the University of Colorado Denver, who served as the lead researcher in the aforementioned meditation study. "It allows you to mentally set aside your burden for a brief respite."[58]

Furthermore, prayer has the potential to nurture a sense of connection—with a higher power, one's surroundings, and fellow individuals, including "the preceding generations of individuals who have engaged in prayer," remarks Kevin Ladd, a psychologist and the director of the Social Psychology of Religion Lab at Indiana University South Bend.[59]

Individuals engage in prayer for different reasons: seeking guidance, expressing gratitude, finding solace, or seeking protection. However, not all prayer holds equal significance, according to experts. A study conducted in 2004, focusing on religious coping methods and published in the Journal of Health Psychology, revealed that individuals who perceive God as a partner or collaborator in their lives tend to experience enhanced mental and physical well-being. Conversely, those who harbor anger towards God, feeling punished or abandoned, or those who relinquish personal responsibility and rely solely on God for solutions tend to experience poorer outcomes. Dr. Pargament, the principal researcher of the study, likens this phenomenon to the positive influence of a loving relationship with a partner, which brings out the best in an individual.[60]

I'm sorry I had to bring scientific research into this; it's just part of who I am. Yet, no matter the "scientific evidence," there is no denying that spiritual strength through prayer is a profound and transformative experience that has been practiced across cultures and religions for centuries. Prayer, as a form of communication with God, holds the potential to nourish the spirit, cultivate inner strength, and provide solace during

---

58   Ídem.
59   Ídem.
60   Ídem.

challenging times. It serves as a powerful tool for us to connect with our spiritual essence and find guidance, peace, and resilience.

This is what Karola would do for hours and hours when she was held captive. She would pray. She still does, and she describes her relationship with God and the presence of God in her life as the reason she is where and how she is today. God saved her in more ways than one.

Prayer shifts everything, and although it is a deeply personal and introspective practice, it allows us to express, in our own particular way, our deepest desires, concerns, gratitude, and aspirations to God. Through prayer, we don't only communicate our needs and hopes but also listen attentively for messages, insights, and guidance. Through this exchange, we find comfort in knowing that we are not alone in our journey and, better yet, that there is a higher power that can offer support and understanding.

So, even for some of us who need to include science in our lives, prayer and connection to God do not discriminate; they only foster our spiritual strength and cultivate a sense of connection and belonging. We are able to acknowledge our relationship with God and recognize His place in the grand tapestry of existence. This connection instills a sense of purpose, meaning, and significance in our lives. It allows us to transcend our immediate circumstances and gain a broader perspective on life's challenges and opportunities.

Moreover, prayer acts as a catalyst for self-reflection and personal growth. By engaging in regular prayer, we are encouraged to examine our thoughts, emotions, and actions with greater awareness. We have the opportunity to align our intentions and behaviors with higher values and principles, leading to a deeper understanding of ourselves and our place in the world. Through introspection and self-correction, we can cultivate virtues such as patience, compassion, forgiveness, and gratitude, which contribute to our spiritual well-being and strength.

Prayer also provides a sanctuary of peace and solace amidst the turbulence of life. When Karola told me how she would pray, I visualized her in the terrible situation she experienced with a light surrounding her. I can't fathom how she did it, pray, I mean, yet at the same time, I fully understand it. She found, through the most difficult of times, a safe space to express her pain, fears, and worries while also being open to receiving divine healing, strength, and guidance. She surrendered, and she trusted.

This surrender was an openness to divine wisdom. By letting go and having faith, she found the strength to endure the worst of times, persevere in the face of unbelievable adversity, and embrace life's unfolding journey with grace and resilience.

Prayer nourishes the spirit; it allows us to walk down a transformative pathway that empowers us to tap into our inner resources and experience the presence of the divine in our lives. Prayer, my dear readers, is a gift.

And through prayer, we can also connect with our hope, which gives us a sense of purpose, resilience and meaning, and bonds us to our faith. Our faith, in turn, provides solace during challenging times and inspires us to persevere, even in the most difficult moments, instilling in us the belief that there is light at the end of the tunnel, even when circumstances seem bleak. With hope, we find the courage to face challenges head-on, maintain a positive outlook, and pursue solutions. It contributes to our mental and emotional well-being, offering a sense of optimism, reducing stress and anxiety, and providing a foundation for emotional resilience. By having faith, we find comfort, inner peace, and a sense of connectedness to something beyond ourselves.

We also find guidance, values, and principles that shape our choices, relationships, and personal growth. We find inspiration to live with intention and contribute positively to our communities and the world. Coping with loss and grief is a little bit easier because we end up understanding and accepting the natural cycle of life as well as the uncertainties of existence.

For Karola, hope and spiritual faith fueled her resilience and perseverance. They reminded her that what she was living was not permanent and provided her with divine support and guidance. With this, she was able to continue to put one foot in front of the other, one day at a time, and at such an early age, understand the inherent worth and dignity of all beings, which has led to her acts of kindness, forgiveness, love, and passion for social justice.

Karola's faith gives me hope and reminds me, yet again, that everything is possible. We can contribute to building a more compassionate and harmonious world, and the beautiful thing is that we can do it together.

CHAPTER 14:

2000

A new year and a new millennium...we remember. George Bush became president, the movie *Gladiator* was released and would go to win the Academy Award for Best Picture, "O," Oprah's magazine was released, Destiny's Child conquered the charts, the world didn't end with Y2K, and with the help of the Interpol, the Mexican police was able to find them on January 13, 2000.

The New York Times article by Julia Preston published January 14, 2000, Section A, Page 12,

Mexican Star in Sex Case Is Arrested in Rio

The last time that the pop star ██████████ performed on television in Mexico, she pranced and tossed her mane of wavy hair with the carefree defiance that made her an icon of rebellion among young girls.

Today the artist was back on television again. Looking subdued and wearing a gray T-shirt in place of her old sequined halter top, ██████ was caught by cameras in Rio de Janeiro, where she was arrested on charges of corrupting minors that are pending against her here.

██████ longtime manager, ████████████████, was also arrested, along with another singer in the case, ████ ██████████. ██████████ is accused of forcing sex on young girls who were among his teenage protegees.

He and ██████, 29, dropped from view over a year ago. They have been fugitives since arrest warrants were issued here in November. Mexico immediately initiated extradition proceedings today. In statements to the police in Brazil, ██████ and ██████ denied the charges.

The scandal has burned hot for months, exposing the underside of an insular entertainment world filled with freewheeling sex, where ██████████ had gained the mesmerizing power of a cult leader with young girls who hoped for stardom.

Although ███████ became one of Mexico's flashiest stars in the early 90's because of her image of independence, a number of girls who said they had been lured into ████████ harem have contended that the singer was utterly dominated by him and that she helped him commit sexual abuse.

The charges against ███████ and ███████, whose real name is ████████████, were first brought by the parents of ████████████ whose family sent her to study piano at a school run by ██████████ when she was 12. In 1997, when she was 15, ████████, who was living in Spain with ████████, ████████ and six other girls, gave birth to a boy. Miss Yapor abandoned the emaciated infant in a Spanish hospital, and her parents finally took him into their care in Mexico.

In their criminal complaint, ████████ parents contended that ████████ had kidnapped their daughter and fathered her baby by force.

On Dec. 16, ████████, who had not been home in two years, suddenly turned up here at the studios of ██████, the national network where ████████ had been a star. In interviews so wooden that she seemed to be speaking from a memorized text, ████████ called on her parents to drop the charges against ██ and ████████.

She offered her celebrity associates a "very big apology, because they were always very nice to me," and denied that the rock manager was the father of her child.

But ████████ then returned to her parents' home in northern Chihuahua state and made no further statements, and her family did not drop the charges. At least four other young women have testified to the police since ████████ case became public that ████████ had hit them and forced them to have sex with him as a condition for continuing with his music training.

"God always brings justice, both in heaven and on earth," ████ ████████ father, ██████, said in a telephone interview today. But ████████ said it was not clear whether his daughter would testify against ████████ in the trial.

A version of this article appears in print on Jan. 14, 2000, Section

A, Page 12 of the National edition with the headline: Mexican Star in Sex Case Is Arrested in Rio.[61]

The young woman later retracted her statement and admitted that her son was Antonio's. I can only imagine the fear she felt and the manipulation and coercion she experienced to make this statement...because that is what Karola experienced.

The Los Angeles Times also wrote about that day,

Mexican Pop Star ███████,
Manager Arrested in Sex Scandal

L.A. TIMES ARCHIVES

JAN. 14, 2000 12 AM PT

REUTERS

RIO DE JANEIRO—

Mexican pop star ███████ was arrested Thursday by Brazilian police for possible extradition to Mexico to face allegations that she and her manager kidnapped girls and abused them.

███ and manager ███████ were found in a modest apartment at Rio's famous Copacabana beach, an official said.

In Mexico, a state prosecutor for the northern state of Chihuahua, who issued a warrant for ███ arrest in November, said the charges against her and ███ were rape, kidnapping and corruption of minors.

Interpol had been trying for several months to track down ███ and ███, who were believed to be on the run together in Latin America. They were rumored to be in Brazil in mid-1999, but federal police at that time said they had no leads.

The two disappeared after allegations surfaced in early 1999 that ███ had exploited young girls sent by their parents into the pop star's care in hopes of making it big in show business.

---

61   Preston, Julia. "Mexican Star in Sex Case Is Arrested in Rio." The New York Times, January 14, 2000. https://www.nytimes.com/2000/01/14/world/mexican-star-in-sex-case-is-arrested-in-rio.html.

Families of victims later told reporters that the girls were pressured into having sex with ███████.

███, 29, became a star in the early 1990s, rising to the top of the music charts and gaining a reputation as a rebel by appearing on stage in skimpy outfits and pouring soft drinks over her body.[62]

I could go on and on with different articles that came out about that day, but I think you get the idea. Just as news articles and TV shows were talking about this constantly, the victim's faces were all over the mass media. Everyone knew their names, what they looked like, and certain details about what they had lived. The media, as it has happened so many times, cruelly and in self-interest exploited these stories as much as they could without taking into account the effect it was all having on the lives of these young women. Something else I find amazing, both in a shocking and sad way and then in a hopefully good way, is that in the year 2000, there were no laws against human trafficking in Mexico.

Karola remembers it like it was yesterday. Antonio and Laura left to go to the market or something like that, leaving the girls in the different apartments "by themselves." They were so manipulated, threatened, and coerced that the way it worked was that some of the girls were in "higher rank" and would watch over the others. Yet that day, a Thursday like any other, the first thing Karola did when she woke up was pray. She remembers because it was a very particular prayer and she wasn't used to praying in the morning. It was as if this divine intuitive connection led her to utter pleas of mercy in a different way than she ever had. She pictured Jonathan's beautiful brown eyes that she had consciously memorized, and instead of focusing her energy on missing him, she prayed to God to envelop him in light. She prayed for her sisters, for her baby niece, and for the other victims. She prayed for a miracle.

That day, Antonio and Laura did not return; they were taken into custody. There is an interview where Laura says that she honestly thought they would let her go that night. The footage that was taken of the arrest shows Laura blowing kisses and waving to the camera; I kid you not.

---

62 "Mexican Pop Star ███████, Manager Arrested in Sex Scandal." Los Angeles Times, January 14, 2000. https://www.latimes.com/archives/la-xpm-2000-jan-14-mn-53975-story.html.

Oblivious to what had happened, Karola heard a knock so heavy that it reverberated through the door, echoing through the apartment. The subsequent silence was almost palpable—something was happening. A series of knocks repeated, a combination of aggression and insistence. The knocks continued until the police entered the apartment, breaking the boundary that separated two distinct worlds. The police rescued the girls, and some were taken into custody. It was a while until Karola saw Jonathan; he was staying in another apartment. When she was finally able to hold him in her arms, she remembered his gaze, wide with curiosity and innocence, as she held him closer to inhale his sweet scent as if to remember the moment forever. He was swathed in tattered and worn rags yet looked more beautiful than ever. It was the first time in her life she cried tears of joy, and as if a veil was lifted through these tears, she gazed into her son's eyes and saw a future of possibilities.

They took several of the victims to a hotel and started emitting all of the documents needed to get them home: birth certificates for the babies and passports for their mothers. They ordered food for them, and Karola remembers the taste of that hamburger to perfection. She had never been so hungry; each bite was submerged with anticipation, gratitude, and disbelief that food was finally within her reach.

As the adrenaline settled, her hunger was satisfied, and her baby was in her arms, a profound fatigue enveloped her like a heavy shroud. She was finally able to feel her exhaustion and the right to give her body the rest she needed. She slept next to her baby, holding him tight, sighing in relief and disbelief; this was one of the best moments of her life.

Karola has told me several times that it was the love for her son and the power of prayer that saved her. Her son's life gave her a reason not to give up, to keep having hope, to have faith, and to feel gratitude.

So many things happened all at once, and without understanding how, the faces of Antonio, Laura, and all of their victims were all over the news. Imagine not having access to any form of communication for years…no television, no radio, no newspapers, and then, with access to it, what you hear and see constantly is your face. They were referred to as a clan, and although there were divided opinions at the time about what had happened, that continues to this day. Antonio, Laura, Jane, and some of the other victims were taken to jail. Karola was able to go home. One of her sisters was put in jail in Mexico, in Chihuahua, which is a State in

Mexico far away from their native Puebla. She had to go to help her sister get out of jail. Her parents were in such a state of devastation that my heart goes out to them even twenty-three years later.

Karola made her first statement in a court of law on October 24, 2000, and she did so to provide information pertinent to what they had all experienced. She mentioned that she didn't give her statement before then because she had been manipulated and brainwashed on what to say to her family and the authorities. She had received letters from Antonio with instructions—letters that she corresponded in a loving manner, even sending pictures of her and Jonathan. She feared for her life and her son's life. She had been enslaved by two of the most famous people in Mexico and feared that the moment they would be released, they would come after her and her son.

When she slowly began to understand that they really were behind bars and there might be justice for what they had done to so many young women, things began to change for her. She had been isolated from other people for so long that there was a part of her that had normalized her everyday life and the torture that went with it. She was scared, in shock, and experiencing posttraumatic stress. She had somehow accepted the idea that living in slavery was her only option. Antonio's words were on repeat in her thoughts, "Nobody ever beats me," "You will never leave," and it took a very long time to drown them out.

When she was finally free and back with her parents, she realized it had all been lies, manipulation, torture, and gaslighting and that what controlled her was fear. She couldn't bear the thought of being separated from her son again. Yet, even though fear began to slowly fade, every time she would think of speaking up, her narrative, stolen by the media, haunted her. She was humiliated, abused, and felt profoundly broken, yet in the midst of the most intense inner turmoil, she would turn around and look at her son and instantly smile. Jonathan was a gift from God; he transformed her life, her faith, her strength, and her resilience. Jonathan's existence paved the way to her joy, to the ineffable experience of true love, the love of a mother to her child.

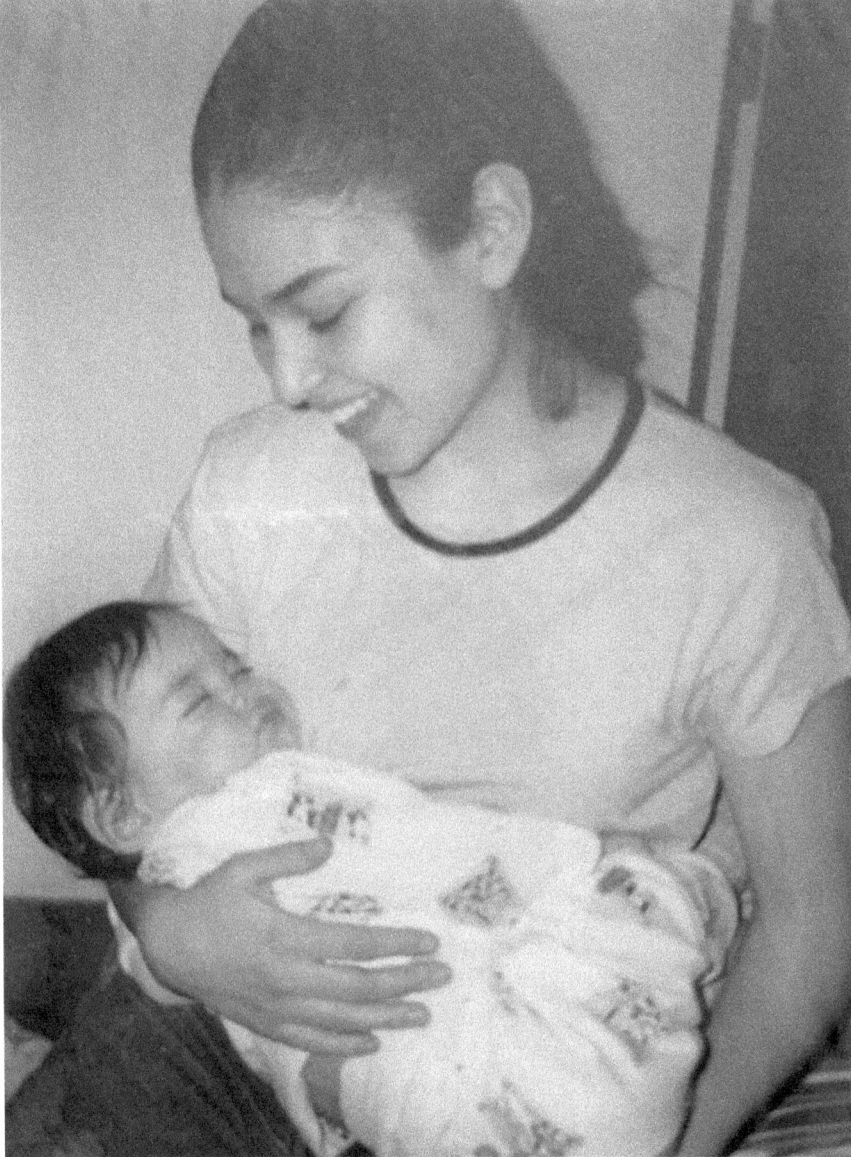

Karola pictured with her son at the end of the year 2000.

"Truly I tell you, if you have faith as small as a mustard seed, you can say to this mountain, 'Move from here to there,' and it will move. Nothing will be impossible for you" (Matthew 17:20, NIV).

CHAPTER 15:
Gaslighting

The term gaslighting comes from a 1938 play by Patrick Hamilton, known in America as *Angel Street*, and later developed into the film *Gas Light* by Alfred Hitchcock.

In the suspense film, a manipulative husband tries to make his wife think she is losing her mind by making subtle changes in her environment, including dimming the flame on a gas lamp little by little. Not only does he disrupt her environment and make her believe she is insane, but he also abuses and controls her, cutting her off from family and friends.[63]

Gaslighting is a form of manipulation or emotional abuse that often occurs in abusive relationships. The bully or abuser misleads the target, creating a false narrative and making them question their judgments and reality.[64] What ends up happening is that the victim of gaslighting starts to feel insecure and unsure about their perceptions of the world and can even wonder if they are losing their sanity.

Gaslighting usually takes place over an extended period of time and causes the victim to question the validity of their own thoughts, perception of reality, or even memories. This can lead to loss of confidence and self-esteem, confusion, and uncertainty of one's mental stability. What results commonly is a dependency on the perpetrator. Gaslighting tends to occur primarily in romantic relationships, yet is not uncommon in controlling friendships or family relationships. People who gaslight may have mental disorders and use this type of emotional abuse to exert power over others to manipulate them, using this technique to undermine the other's perception of reality.[65]

When someone is gaslighting you, you may second-guess yourself, your memories, recent events, and perceptions. It looks like communicating with

63   Thomas, Laura. "Gaslight and Gaslighting - the Lancet Psychiatry." The Lancet Psychiatry, February 2018. https://www.thelancet.com/journals/lanpsy/article/PIIS2215-0366(18)30024-5/abstract.

64   Breines J. Call me crazy: The subtle power of gaslighting. *Berkeley Science Review.* April 2012.

65   Gordon, Sherri. "Is Someone Gaslighting You? Learn the Warning Signs." Verywell Mind, n.d. https://www.verywellmind.com/is-someone-gaslighting-you-4147470.

the person who is gaslighting you and being left wondering if there is some-thing wrong with you, that you are to blame for something, or that you are just being too sensitive. It can confuse you and cause you to question your memory, self-worth, judgment, and overall mental health.

There are different tactics used by people who do gaslighting; here are a few:[66]

- Lying: They can blatantly lie and never back down or change their stories, even if you provide proof of it. They may, in turn, say things like, "You're making things up," "That never happened," or "You're crazy." Lying and distortion are the cornerstones of gaslighting behavior. Even when you know they are not telling the truth, they can be very convincing. In the end, you start to second-guess yourself.

- Discrediting you: People who gaslight may spread rumors and gossip about you to others and may pretend to be worried about you while subtly telling others you seem emotionally unstable or "crazy." This tactic can be very effective, and unfortunately, many people side with the abuser without knowing the full story. Something else that can happen is that this person may lie to you, telling you that other people also think this about you even if nobody said anything.

- Distracting you: When asking someone who gaslights a question or you call them out for something they said or did, they may change the subject by asking a question instead of responding to the issue at hand. This causes you to question the need to press the matter or throw off your train of thought.

- Minimizing your thoughts and feelings: Trivializing your emo-tions allows the person who is gaslighting you to gain power over you. They might make statements like: "Calm down," "You're overreacting," or "Why are you so sensitive?" All of these statements minimize how you're feeling or what you're thinking and communicate that you're wrong.[67]

66   Ahern, Kathy. "Institutional Betrayal and Gaslighting: Why Whistle-Blowers Are So Traumatized." The Journal of Perinatal & Neonatal Nursing, 2018. https://journals.lww.com/jpnnjournal/abstract/2018/01000/institutional_betrayal_and_gas-lighting__why.14.aspx.
67   Sweet, Paige L. "The Sociology of Gaslighting." American Sociological Associa-tion, 2019. https://journals.sagepub.com/doi/10.1177/0003122419874843.

- Shifting blame: When every discussion you have is somehow twisted to where you are to blame for something that occurred. Even when you try to discuss how the abuser's behavior makes you feel, they're able to twist the conversation so that you end up questioning if you are the cause of their bad behavior.

- Denying wrongdoing: People who engage in bullying and emotional abuse are notorious for denying that they did anything wrong. They do this to avoid taking responsibility for their poor choices. This denial can leave the victim of gaslighting feeling unseen, unheard, and as though the impact on them is of no importance. This tactic also makes it very hard for the victim to move on or to heal.[68]

- Using compassionate words as weapons: It could occur that when called out or questioned, a person who gaslights will use kind and loving words to try to smooth over the situation. Something along the lines of "You know how much you mean to me; I would never hurt you on purpose." Although it might be something we want to hear if the behavior is repeated, the words are inauthentic, and it is just manipulation.

- Rewriting history: The person gaslighting might retell stories in ways that are in their favor, causing the other person to doubt their memory of what happened.

When dealing with someone who never acknowledges your thoughts, feelings, or beliefs, you may begin to question them yourself. What's more, you may never feel validated or understood, which can be extremely isolating, shaming, and difficult to cope with.

---

68   Kacel EL, Ennis N, Pereira DB. Narcissistic personality disorder in clinical health psychology practice: case studies of comorbid psychological distress and life-limiting illness. *Behav Med.* 2017;43(3):156-164. doi:10.1080/08964289.2017.13 01875MLA.

THE SIGNS

Being subjected to gaslighting can have important consequences; it can cause anxiety, depression, and other mental health concerns, including addiction and thoughts of suicide.[69] Here are some signs of gaslighting:[70]

- Doubting your feelings and reality: Trying to convince yourself that the treatment you receive is not that bad or that you are too sensitive.

- Questioning your judgment and perceptions: Being afraid of expressing your emotions or speaking up, feeling worse after you do, so you choose to stay silent.

- Feeling vulnerable and insecure: Feeling like you have to "walk on eggshells" around that person, as well as feeling on edge and lacking self-esteem.

- Feeling alone and powerless: Being convinced that people around you think you are "crazy" or "strange," as the person who is gaslighting tells you, feeling trapped and isolated.

- Wondering if you are what they say you are: Hearing words about you like inadequate, unintelligent, or insane and wondering if it is true.

- Being disappointed in yourself and who you have become: Feeling weak or passive when you used to be stronger and more assertive.

- Worrying that you are too sensitive: When the person minimizes hurtful behaviors by saying, "It was just a joke" or "You need thicker skin," and you wonder if that is true.

- Having a sense of impending doom: Constantly feeling like something bad is going to happen when you are around that person.

- Spending a lot of time apologizing: Feeling the need to apologize all the time for what you do or who you are.

- Feeling inadequate: Feeling like you are never "good enough" and trying to live up to the expectations and demands of others, even if they are unreasonable.

---

69   Christensen, Martin, and Anne Evans-Murray. "Gaslighting in Nursing Academia: A New or Established Covert Form of Bullying?" Wiley Online Library, May 3, 2021. https://onlinelibrary.wiley.com/doi/10.1111/nuf.12588.
70   Gordon, Sherri. "Is Someone Gaslighting You? Learn the Warning Signs." Verywell Mind, n.d. https://www.verywellmind.com/is-someone-gaslighting-you-4147470.

- **Second-guessing yourself:** Frequently wondering if you accurately remember the details of past events, and might even stop trying to share what you recall for fear of being wrong.

- **Assuming others are disappointed in you:** Constantly apologizing for what you do and who you are, and assuming people are let down by you or that you have somehow made a mistake.

- **Wondering what's wrong with you:** Worrying that you are not well mentally.

- **Struggling to make decisions because you distrust yourself:** Preferring to allow the other person to make decisions for you and avoid decision-making altogether.

If you think you might be experiencing gaslighting in a relationship, it is advisable to talk to a professional who can guide you closely. Here are a couple of suggestions that do not replace a therapeutic process:[71]

- **Gaining some distance:** Taking a step back from the intense emotions gaslighting can generate. You can practice deep breathing and relaxation techniques or physically leave the situation.

- **Saving the evidence:** Since gaslighting makes us question everything, keeping a journal and saving text conversations or emails to go back to can be helpful.

- **Setting boundaries:** Being clear about what you are not willing to allow or accept in a relationship.

- **Getting an outside perspective:** Having conversations with people you trust about what is going on. Having someone else's perspective can be very helpful.

- **Ending the relationship:** Although difficult, ending a relationship with someone who is constantly gaslighting is the most effective way to end the abuse.

Although gaslighting mainly occurs in romantic relationships or in controlling friendships or family relationships, it can also occur through the media. In this day and age, mass and social media play a pivotal role in determining the direction of certain situations. Without a doubt, its critical and influential position has an impact on how we view certain

---

71   Ídem.

matters, including situations that have happened to others. Karola and her family have experienced more than their fair share of gaslighting throughout the years. They have been victims of manipulation and distortion with the intent to undermine their experience, planting seeds of doubt and control over public opinion through the spread of false narratives, the altering of facts, and intentionally presenting information in a way that misleads and confuses.

Of course, in this particular case, with respect to gaslighting, Laura takes the trophy. She has been doing it consistently for over twenty-three years. You see, she has not only done it since they were caught and taken to prison, spreading hate and lies to "prove" her innocence, but she has been downplaying Karola's situation, as well as the situation of every other victim since they were under their reign. "It's not that bad," "He cares for you," "You wanted it to happen," "Jonathan is allegedly Antonio's son." This last example, which is written in one of Laura's books, shocked me profoundly. Who else's child could Jonathan be? Karola was enslaved for years, raped by the same man every time he felt like it since she was thirteen years old. She was locked in a room, had no access to the outside world, was beaten, starved, prohibited from speaking to other people, forced to have an abortion, transported illegally into the United States, and subjected to forced labor. She wasn't asking for it, for any of it. Yet, if we were so brainwashed or ignorant as to actually believe that, there is a slight fact that turns everything around: she was a minor. Laura was twenty-eight years old, and Antonio was forty-one when Karola was thirteen. I'm not very good at math, but even my dog would be able to figure this one out. Antonio tortured Karola and the other victims during the years they were their slaves. Laura has terrorized Karola and the other victims until this very day.

With respect to sexual intercourse, as Laura said in an interview in the early 2000s, implying Karola and her sister enjoyed it, I wished the interviewer would have responded the following, "*She was a minor. This is a crime.*"

For the record, which I am almost sure is crystal clear, dear readers, Karola did not enjoy any minute she was a slave; she was repulsed and fractured to her very core by that experience. Whoever suggests or believes otherwise either lacks basic common sense or is extremely evil. I see no other options.

CHAPTER 15: GASLIGHTING

THE IMPACT OF THE MEDIA ON REVICTIMIZATION

We have seen it so many times before. Princess Dianna, Britney Spears, Pamela Anderson...the media documenting the most difficult moments of people's lives for others' entertainment.

In the US alone, there are more than 32,000 broadcast radio and TV stations, along with hundreds of cable TV and satellite radio stations. On top of that, we have daily newspapers, magazines targeting all kinds of readers, and, of course, the immeasurable breadth of the internet. Currently, we have more ways to reach more people than we've ever had in the history of humankind.[72]

Without a doubt, there are many pros to living in a hyperconnected world. It can keep us connected, spur business, spread art and culture, and give a voice to the voiceless, among other things. Among the many cons, it can empower the already powerful, homogenize culture, overtake personal connections, and a very particular one that has caused severe harm: it can be used for disinformation and hate.

In Karola's case, the latter had an impact. Media outlets portrayed her nightmare in a morbid tone of consensual sexual orgies involving her and her sisters, as well as blaming her and her parents for all that happened. Victim-blaming is holding a victim at least partially responsible for what happened to them. Public opinion may reject the notion that they are innocent victims and instead blame them for not preventing their victimization.[73] Harmful, sexist views can normalize the notion that men can have uncontrollable sexual urges and that women should take extra precautions not to arouse them through their appearance or behavior. Victim-blaming suggests that women are gatekeepers of male desire and are expected to endure male aggression.[74]

Revictimization means to victimize someone again. It is a crushing reality that the digital sphere has become a space in which misogyny-laden

---

72   "The Pros And Cons Of Mass Media." Walden University, n.d. https://www.waldenu.edu/online-bachelors-programs/bs-in-communication/resource/the-pros-and-cons-of-mass-media.
73   Digidiki, Vasileia, Baka, Aphrodite. "Who's to Blame in the Sex Trafficking of Women: Situational and Individual Factors that Define a 'Deserving Victim.'" Journal of Human Trafficking, 2022.
74   Casarella-Espinoza, Michelle. "Whose Fault Is It Anyway? Comparison of Victim Blaming Attitudes Towards Sex Trafficking and Sexual Assault Across Gender and Two Ethnic Groups," 2015.

FAITH, LOVE AND HUMAN TRAFFICKING

discourses are constantly presented. In the article "Rape Culture, Revictimization, and Social Representations: Images and Discourses on Sexual and Violent Crimes in the Digital Sphere in Mexico," published in Sage Journals, the authors discuss how the persistent rape culture that is normalized in Mexico tends to justify violent acts against women, blaming the victims through social opinions.[75] They proposed an approach based on the theory of social representations, with the objective of analyzing the discourses that emerge in the digital sphere when users give their opinion on five types of crimes against women: femicide, rape, enforced disappearance, abuse, and sexual harassment. The results revealed that there are four types of discourse framed within rape culture: disbelief of rape, blaming the victim, revictimization, and disempowering women, concluding that Mexican society maintains a representation that stereotypes and devalues the image of women, which allows us to understand the aggressions that women suffer in their daily lives.

In all honesty, this comes as no surprise in a country where you are a target because of your gender.

Adding to the trauma and pain that victims experience through sexual abuse, many times, it is relived when victims reveal what happened to them. This makes the experience exponentially more difficult because, in addition to the actual abuse, other people or groups of people contribute to the trauma by inquiring into too many intimate details and being tactless. In addition to the physical consequences of sexual abuse, the psychological impact is enormous. Reliving and perpetuating the facts in the mind of a survivor of sexual abuse can cause, in addition to negative emotions and thoughts, self-blame and isolation, as well as trigger psychological problems and psychophysiological disorders such as:

- Post-traumatic stress.
- Substance abuse.
- Loss of motivation and self-esteem.
- Depressive symptoms.

---

75   Reyes-Sosa, Hiram, Sonia Martínez-Cueva, and Nahia Idoiaga Mondragón. "Rape Culture, Revictimization, and Social Representations: Images and Discourses on Sexual and Violent Crimes in the Digital Sphere in Mexico." Sage Journals, April 1, 2021. https://journals.sagepub.com/.

- Anxiety.
- Difficulties concentrating.
- Constant fear.
- Feelings of anger and injustice.
- Isolation or avoidance behavior.
- Suicidal ideation.
- Sleep disorders.
- Psychosomatic illnesses.
- Headaches.
- Cardiovascular and/or gastrointestinal effects.

Revictimization has countless effects on the victim, and if the person is exposed to guilt and stigmatization and is constantly subjected to having their dignity violated time and time again, the healing process becomes more difficult, which is many times the reason why survivors of sexual abuse prefer to remain silent and carry these heavy burdens alone.[76]

There are ways to reduce victimization and revictimization:

- Respect the victim's identity.
- Avoid justifying the violent act.
- Validate their emotions.
- Reduce the length of legal proceedings.

When people don't listen to survivors, it makes it less likely that others will come forward. It also makes it less likely that survivors will seek the kind of mental health support they need. This can have serious consequences.

According to RAINN:[77]

- Ninety-four percent of women who are raped experience symptoms of PTSD during the two weeks following rape.

---

76   "How Does Revictimization Occur and How to Avoid It?" Yo digo no más, n.d. https://yodigonomas.com/en/blog/how-does-revictimization-occur-and-how-to-avoid-it/.
77   "Victims of Sexual Violence: Statistics." RAINN, n.d. https://www.rainn.org/statistics/victims-sexual-violence.

- Thirty percent of women who are raped still experience PTSD symptoms nine months later.

- Thirty-three percent of women who've been raped have contemplated suicide.

- Thirteen percent of women who've been raped have attempted suicide.

That level of trauma—especially when left untreated—can damage not just physical and emotional health but many aspects of life.

Karola, along with her sisters and parents, found themselves entangled in a web of deceit, their stories distorted and their pain brushed aside. The correspondence she exchanged with Antonio at the beginning was exposed in an interview with international reach, leaving her with nothing but shame and doubt about her part in what had happened. She was a child; she was coerced, she was terrified, she was manipulated and brainwashed. The corrosive aftermath of their experience, added to the heart-wrenching accusation of blame, became a profoundly disturbing chapter in their journey toward healing.

Power gave its possessors the ability to reshape reality to suit their own agendas. In the face of accountability, those involved were able to paint a different picture of half-truths and confusion, feeding a pattern of denial, revictimization, and manipulation. The intricate details of Karola's narrative were twisted and molded, her voice silenced, and her experiences dismissed as lies or attempts to gain fame she never wanted.

The act of denial became a dangerous weapon, twisting the truth of the shared reality of many. What should have been a safe space for Karola and her parents to seek solace and justice was instead transformed into an arena where their pain was belittled and their truth obscured. This served to amplify their suffering, leaving some scars deeper than the wounds themselves, as if the weight of everything that had happened wasn't heavy enough. Their vulnerability, already exposed by the traumas they endured, was exploited, leaving them feeling defenseless against the onslaught of power and manipulation. Their stories were reduced to mere whispers, drowned out by the media. The very foundation of their mental health was shaken, and the seeds of doubt that had been planted began to take root, casting shadows on their ability to trust, believe, and find closure. The depth of the injustice is difficult to understand from the outside; from the inside, it was a stain on their path to healing that cast a darkness over their attempts to reclaim their narrative.

Can you imagine, dear readers, what it was like for a seventeen-year-old with a baby whose face was all over the news, whose name and sister's names were everywhere, to go out to the street? Can you imagine what it was like to be told by strangers that she asked for it or to have strangers blame her parents for what happened to her? Can you imagine the humiliation? The profound sadness? The anger? Now, add fear for your life and your child's life to the mix. That was just the tip of the iceberg.

As I mentioned earlier, Laura wrote a book that came out in 2002 while she was still in jail, talking about the story of her life, her rise to success, and the sex scandal that led to her downfall. In this book, she mentions many of the victims, including Karola. She not only mentions them by name, but provides pictures of them. When talking about Karola, Laura mentions that she wrote love letters to Antonio while they were in jail and implied that her son was not Antonio's. She mentioned them both by name, and the picture in this part shows not only Karola's face but also her son's.

In an interview done in September 2000, Laura was asked if she had any knowledge of any of the girls having an abortion or if, at any time, any of them asked her for advice. Her answer was a definitive no. In this same interview, the interviewer mentions Karola and her sisters by name, showing their faces as they were walking out the door when the police found them, two of them carrying their babies.[78]

I can't understand, for the life of me, what Laura was thinking about adding a picture of two minors *without consent*, implying that Jonathan was Antonio's "alleged" son. She was there; she knew the only man there was Antonio; she took part and witnessed everything that happened to every single girl who was lured into that life with the promise to be part of her entourage. Laura, Karola, and one of Karola's sisters had Antonio's children in a lapse of about six months. Bullying the victims, exposing their faces, and claiming she is innocent is like Cruella De Vil claiming she wears faux fur when we all know she has Dalmatian blood on her hands.

Everyone is entitled to claim their innocence; it is the cornerstone of justice and a fundamental human right. What everyone is not entitled to

---

78   Candiani, Ana Patricia. "   Especial de Ocurrió Así." YouTube, January 18, 2021. https://www.youtube.com/watch?v=vLTf0ELN7m8&t=1424s.

is exposing minors by name and image without consent, which is an invasion of privacy and defamation. Exposing them like this proves nothing; it did disclose them, putting even more attention on them in the public sphere when the only thing Karola wanted was peace within her freedom.

Image of Karola and her son in Laura's book.

CHAPTER 16:
2001 – 2003

Things change from one moment to the next, and the first years of the new millennium were immersed in ongoing change. On September 11, 2001, our world, as we knew it, changed. All around the world, we watched horrified as a series of coordinated terrorist attacks took place in the United States. Extreme collective fear and anger took over, and at the same time, the number of distractions we had continued to grow. *Harry Potter* films, *Lord of the Rings* trilogy, Michael Jackson dangling his son from a window, Michael Jordan retired, reality shows, iPods, iTunes, Space Shuttles, questionable fashion trends like low-rise jeans, tattoo choker necklaces, and trucker hats. Technology was hard to keep up with. Apple unveiled the web browser Safari, WordPress.org was released, Tesla Motors was founded, and Skype was launched. The most popular websites were Yahoo, AOL, MSN, Microsoft, eBay, Google, Go.com, Netscape, Windows Media, and Weather.com. Last but not least, President Bush signed The Controlling the Assault of Non-Solicited Pornography and Marketing (CAN-SPAM) Act into law. These events, among many, many others, marked the first years of the new millennium. Honestly, looking back, it was a whirlwind. Things were changing so fast that most of us could barely keep up. Things were changing exponentially for Karola as well.

Many interviews of Laura, Antonio, and Jane took place during these years while they were in jail in Brazil. Among the different ones I came across, I want to share the one from New York Times Magazine.[79]

By Christopher McDougall

April 6, 2002

For a woman who had spent the past 25 months in a Brazilian prison, using a hole in the floor for a toilet and a knee-high spigot for a shower, ███████ looked magnificent.

It was February in the Hospital Regional da Saúde da Asa Norte, in Brasília, and the Mexican pop star was propped up by pillows in bed, flanked by two enormous bouquets of roses. Her

79   Mcdougall, Christopher. "Slick Transit ███." The New York Times, April 6, 2002. https://www.nytimes.com/2002/04/06/magazine/slick-transit-███.html.

eyes were shadowed, her lips were glossed and the ███████, or ████████████ that gave a title to both her hit single and her hit movie was brushed out across her chest. Except for her very obvious pregnancy -- and the two federal police officers guarding her door -- ███ could have easily segued into a photo shoot for one of her pinup calendars.

She got out of bed and dragged a steel chair over to the window, where she was now backlit by the afternoon sun. She draped her hair to one side, changed her mind, and arranged it forward again. Hair, makeup, lighting -- perfect. All this stage-management was bewildering -- she was under guard in a hospital, after all -- but effective in at least one way: she looked a decade younger than her 34 years (she claims to be 32) and unmarked by either the ordeal she'd been through or the one that was rapidly approaching: later this spring, ███ could be sent home to face accusations of rape and kidnapping in what would undoubtedly be Mexico's Trial of the Century.

"That is why I'm naming my baby ███████████," ███ said, caressing her belly. "So God will give him wings to fly away from all these troubles."

███████████ has been the biggest name in Mexican entertainment for more than a decade, the multi platinum singer who brought Girl Power to Mexico and made herself an idol to millions of Latin American teenagers. Following her debut album in 1989, the "Mexican Madonna" became a sensation whose every project -- movies, calendars, TV specials, a magazine devoted to all things ███ -- both provoked and sold tremendously well.

███mania was so intense, in fact, that authorities were slow to react when stories began circulating in the late 90's that something dark was going on with all those young girls in her entourage. Rumor had it that her manager, ██████████, was the head of a sex cult that abducted teenage girls. ███ was ██████████ henchwoman, some whispered; others claimed that for all her wealth and she-devil stage antics, ███ was actually just ██████ submissive pet.

But by the time the police set out to sort the villains from the victims in 1999, ███ and ███ had vanished. For more than a year, while the Mexican courts fielded accusations against ███ and ███ of rape, statutory rape, kidnapping and corruption of minors, one of the most recognized icons in Latin America was invisible.

Finally, in January 2000, the police located ███ and ███ in Brazil, in a beachfront apartment on Rio de Janeiro's Copacabana, along with three teenage sisters and ███████████████, a bandmate of ███ known as ███████. The teenagers were returned to Mexico, and the three fugitives have been locked up while Brazil wrestles with Mexico's extradition request.

"It's all false," ███ said tearfully when we met just before she gave birth. "Not a gram of truth." The scandalous claims, she said, have been nothing more than a conspiracy by television-industry enemies and a gold rush by "girls who make book deals, and tell five versions of the same story, and appear on television with long nails and jewelry and new clothes, and can suddenly pay off their houses."

███ promised me she would answer any question -- except one. She would not explain how, after a year in an all-women's cellblock, she somehow got pregnant. And that child could set ███ free: thanks to longstanding custom, Brazil has never extradited the mother of a child born on Brazilian soil. That leaves the Brazilian Supreme Court confronting a difficult decision: respect Mexican wishes and send ███ home, or respect national custom and turn her loose.

"Sometimes God writes straightforward in twisted lines," ███ said. She smiled, wiped her tears, rearranged her hair. "This baby I am expecting is Scripture directly from heaven."

Either ███ lawyers nor the Brazilian police have much use for divine intervention as an explanation. The lawyers claimed -- and still do -- that ███ was raped by prison guards. The police, on the other hand, insisted that ███ had impregnated herself with the sperm of ███████, a notorious Brazilian gangster in the men's cellblock, near ███. According to the police report, ███ chose ███ because he was marked for death, sure to be shanked in prison for having tortured and raped a rival's 3-year-old daughter. With ▮ gone, ▮ would never have to worry about him turning up as a free man and pressing a claim on the family fortune.

The police report claimed that plastic baggies of ▮ semen were smuggled to ▮ inside glasses of warm milk, thereby keeping it roughly at body temperature. ▮ then inseminated herself with a syringe she had constructed from a ballpoint pen. Borelli himself told IstoE, a respected Brazilian newsmagazine, that he was the mystery child's father. He said he sent ▮ at least five bags of semen.

Police suggested ▮ meant to follow the lead of Ronnie Biggs, the Briton who robbed a train in 1963 and then spent nearly another 30 years free in Rio after fathering a child with a Brazilian showgirl in 1974. Biggs became an immediate folk hero in Brazil, thanks to the former colony's soft spot for outlaws, and his son was given a starring role on a children's television program.

▮ lawyers angrily denied all this. They insisted that prison guards raped her, then later tried to kill her and ▮ as a coverup. As evidence, they noted that ▮ was beaten nearly to death by his fellow prisoners one night when his cell was inexplicably left unlocked. The day ▮ returned from the hospital, a burning mattress was stuffed inside his cell, starting a fire that severely burned him and, according to ▮ lawyers, filled the nearby women's cells with choking smoke. "There are people in that prison who have something to hide," said Geraldo Magela, one of ▮ lawyers. "They don't care if they have to burn the prison down to hide it."

The Supreme Court conducted a special hearing, but ▮ said she was in too much danger to reveal the father's identity. She refused even to confirm her lawyers' account that she had been raped. The reason for her secrecy? Wealth and vulnerability, she said. As long as she remained in prison, she was at the mercy of the guards; once she was released, the child's father could claim that the sex was consensual and argue for partial custody. If she died, he would then have a claim to her money. So she wasn't talking.

The Brazilian police, however, tried another means of testing her story. On the day I was at the hospital to interview ███, her lawyer ███ and I stopped to chat with the hospital director in his office. Suddenly three men appeared in the doorway. One flipped open a police ID, then squared his hands on his hips, pushing back his suit jacket to reveal the pistol holstered on his waist.

"We need an extraction of amniotic fluid from ███," the officer said, apparently assuming that the lawyer and I were hospital staff. "Don't tell her what it's for. We want to perform verifiable DNA testing on the child before it's born."

"Ay ya!" ███ exclaimed as he hauled his bulk off the sofa. "Absolutely not! That's unconstitutional! It's an invasion of her privacy."

"You want an invasion?" the officer said. "I've got a van full of cops outside. We'll take this hospital by force if we have to." Cellphones materialized and everyone started dialing. ███ hit the Supreme Court on his speed dial; the hospital director, shaken, called the minister of health. Soon, ███ cried out -- Ha!" -- and handed his cellphone to one of the cops. The court had granted a stay. The cop slapped the cellphone into ███ hand and led his partners out.

"Oh, my God," ███ moaned, then repeated himself victoriously: "O! Deus! Meu!" His elation was short-lived, though; by the time we got to ███ room, he was preoccupied again by her legal fight. The problem is, there's no solid barrier to her immediate extradition, since the law that spared Ronnie Biggs has since been taken off the books. Now it's just a matter of sentiment -- albeit a powerful one -- as the Brazilian government has broadly hinted. "There was obviously a failure in police procedures, and now it will be much more complicated to extradite her," a Justice Ministry spokesman, Djalma Nascimento Jr., told the Brazilian press in the fall, after ███ pregnancy was revealed. "The child will be a Brazilian citizen and therefore cannot be extradited. And it is difficult to imagine extraditing the parent without her child."

███ might win even more sympathy if she were to do what everyone has been expecting: separate herself from ███

[*Antonio]. Almost no one has spoken up on his behalf -- including his brother, ███████, a powerful Mexican senator -- and ████████ few public statements have been disastrous. In one interview he admitted to having sex with a 13-year-old girl; in another he conceded that he might have been a little tough on the girls to make them better performers. (He was unavailable for this article, his lawyers said, because of prison restrictions.)

But ████ has so far remained loyal. When I asked point-blank if ██████ was domineering, she sighed and said: "During a concert once, I was singing ████████████ and because I was dancing so much, my voice started to give out." She managed to hide it, though, by pointing the mike at the crowd and having concertgoers chant the chorus. "When I came offstage, everyone was shouting 'Bravo! Bravo! You are la maxima!'"

Everyone, that is, except ████████. "He looked at me and shook his head. He said, 'It's shameless, to be the highest-paid female performer in Latin America and have your voice go out during a song about █████.' I thought he couldn't tell. But he knew." ████████ woke her up the next morning and made her run 20 times around the town square. "People were watching me, and they were all whispering, 'What an inhuman man, making ████████████ run like that.' But I did it."

As by age 5 she finished the story, █████ sat up straight and threw back her hair. "█████ was a very demanding producer, but they have misinterpreted that brutally," she said firmly. "They have converted him into a kind of hypnotizer. Him into a hypnotizer, and me into some dumb cow. It's all so false. Anything I did, I did because I wanted to. That was the price to be great. Ever since I was 7 years old, I wanted to be great. I knew what I had to do."

By age 5, ████████████████████████████ had mastered a few dance routines, thanks to her mother, a former showgirl who supported the family as a dance teacher. By 7, she was onstage doing local theater in Monterrey, her hometown not far from the Texas border. "The applause just made me crazy," █████ said. "It was all I wanted to do."

The only next step, as every Mexican girl with applause in her ears knows, was to get to Mexico City and fight for a spot in one of the television training academies. When she turned 13, according to ███, she said goodbye to her mother and four younger brothers, ignored her abusive, semi-employed father and set out alone with a single suitcase and a notebook full of her poetry.

"Mexico is probably unlike any other country in the way it develops entertainers," says Sam Quinones, author of the cultural study "True Tales From Another Mexico." Young talent is recruited in the provinces, then taken to Mexico City for years of training at a TV network "star factory." For decades, there was only one network, ███, so competition to get into the performance schools was fierce. The start-up of a second network, ███, in 1993, has only increased the intensity, as the two networks now try to out scout each other by signing up younger and younger performers.

"You don't freelance," Quinones says. "You don't scrounge around like Madonna, hanging out at clubs and hoping for a record deal. The ███ method for creating stars is to seclude young girls in singing and dancing schools, then have them emerge a few years later with a new name and appearance. That's the only way to make it."

Not surprisingly, it's a system ripe for abuse by the men who run it, says Judith Enriqueta Chavez-Parks, the former star known as Ga-Bi. As a 15-year-old backup singer in the mid-70's, she was offered a weekly spot on a Sunday variety show. On her first day of rehearsal, while her mother waited outside, Ga-Bi says she was raped by one of the producers in his office. "That was my first experience as a show-business professional," says Chavez-Parks, who has described the attack in her memoir, "Como Carne de Canon" ("Like Cannon Fodder").

"Like thousands of other girls in Mexico, I kept my mouth shut, because that is what we were always taught to do," says Chavez-Parks, now 42. In 1978, after recording several hits for CBS Records, Ga-Bi was put into the hands of a hot young producer and classically trained pianist, ███. He was very controlling, she says, and not just because of his conservatory background: ███ and his brother, ███, had parents whose discipline touched on the perverse. "His father would whip him, and then his mother would make him get down on his knees, kiss his father's hand and say, 'I love you, Papa,'" Chavez-Parks says.

That upbringing by a domineering father and a submissive mother is Chavez-Parks's only explanation for the path taken by ████. Both brothers seemed to internalize their father's sense of command, but in emphatically different fashions: ████ found his way into politics, while ████ became known as "Mr. Midas" for his knack at turning raw young girls -- and only young girls -- into gold-record singers.

"But he really was a lovely man," Chavez-Parks insists. She has reason to say so: their studio partnership turned into a romance that lasted from 1978 until 1985. It finally ended, she says, because of the teenage girls who had begun following ████ around like groupies. "We were in bed once, and ████ said, 'I've got a girl waiting outside who will do anything we want,'" she recalls. "That's how I met ████ (*Laura)."

After she arrived in Mexico City in 1984, ████ landed a six-month scholarship at the ████ singing academy. On the day it expired, she learned that ████ was putting together a girl group. ████ waited in his office lobby until 2 a.m. for her chance to audition. Then she went berserk, figuring sheer energy was her only chance. It worked. At age 14, ████ became the last girl selected for the five-member group, ████, the ████.

When the ████ disbanded in 1988, ████ approached ████ with some songs she'd written. Her first solo album, ████ made Mexican pop history when three of its singles took over the top three spots on the charts. Everything ████ turned to after that 1989 debut was just as successful -- she sold out stadium concerts and had top-rated TV specials, and her two campy bio-pics, ████ y ████ were among the most popular in the history of Mexican cinema. Her first three albums together sold more than five million copies, and her calendars with seminude photos of the star and her backup singers sold more than a million copies in three years.

A big part of ███ appeal was her image as a sort of anti-Ga-Bi. Suddenly, after decades of saccharine sweethearts, here was a wild thing belting out anthems of teenage freedom. She stripped boys to their underwear onstage and whipped them -- so they'll know how women feel when they're hit," as she has put it. She sang about abortion in her hit ███████ and released an album with the double-entendre title ████████

To Americans jaded by Madonna and Marilyn Manson, a topless girl wearing bandoliers of condoms across her chest may be no more exotic than a tequila commercial, but in a Catholic country with only a single, conservative TV network, ███████ was pure black magic. "The thing about ██████ is she's honest," ████████, a culture critic, has written. "Here's a girl who likes sex and says that it's O.K." People magazine called her "the hottest Latin lover since Valentino."

She became known as ██████, the Bold One. Academics like Carlos Monsivais and journalists like Elena Poniatowska argued that ███ fresh thinking and chaotic self-expression were good for Mexican girlhood. Not that Mexican girlhood needed any encouragement -- ███ imitators were everywhere, with their idol's light-socketed hair and torn party dresses. As the star brought more and more of these ██████ onstage, each concert furthered the impression that she and her army of look-alikes were taking the nation.

The trouble began after ███ brought these star-struck teenagers into her entourage. In 1998, ██████ former publicist, █████ ███, and one of ██████ ex-wives, a young singer named ████████, published ████████." In it they depict ██████ as a wandering pedophile who used ███ concerts as girl-hunting expeditions and made his singers live together in a communal house under his rules. Beatings were delivered for disobedience.

When she was a 13-year-old auditioning for ██████ in 1989, Hernandez says in the book, ███ took her into a side room and told her to strip naked because "we need to see what parts of your body need work." When ██████ grew sick of being just one of ██████ multiple sex partners and threatened to leave, he offered to marry her. They wed in 1990, when she was 15 and he was 34. Although █████ "mesmerized her," she writes, the marriage lasted one month. ████████ returned home to her parents in Mexico City but did not mention the abuse because of "shame and confusion."

████ responded to the book by hitting the talk-show circuit with a vengeance, dismissing ████████ as a jealous singer and bitter divorcee. ████ wasn't romantically involved with ███████, she claimed; she was just speaking up for a good man who happened to be sick with cancer in Europe (which only ████ seemed to know about). "I haven't been 'kidnapped'; far from it, I'm here, I'm sane and I don't belong to any 'satanic cult,'" she said in one TV interview, laughing. "If anyone believes those stories, they're reading too much science fiction." The public believed her, even though ██████ remained out of sight.

But just as the scandal seemed ready to die, a family in Chihuahua received a phone call from Spain. In 1994, ████ and ████████ enrolled their 12-year-old daughter, ████, in ██████ performing-arts school. After ████████ book came out in 1998, ████ disappeared and stopped calling home. The next year, in April, the ████ were notified that their daughter had abandoned a severely malnourished infant at a Madrid hospital. The █████ recovered their grandchild, but Karina was still missing. Her parents filed a criminal complaint in Chihuahua accusing ███ and ████████ of kidnapping and corruption of a minor.

When ████ and ███████ could not be found, an international manhunt was begun. Just months after she'd appeared, giggling, on nationwide TV, ████ was now on a Wanted poster. Several months later, █████ called her parents from Brazil and begged them to drop the charges. They refused, so she and another of ████████ protegees, █████████████, returned to Mexico to plead her case. As soon as they arrived, the 19-year-old █████████ was arrested for kidnapping.

Interpol searched Brazil's visa records and found █████ at an address in Rio. She was gone by the time the police arrived, but she was eventually located a few blocks away, living with ███████,

████████████ and three young sisters. Two of them, both teen-agers, had babies they claimed were ████████. With no charges against them, the three girls were sent home to Mexico, but on their arrival, the eldest was charged with kidnapping and locked up until she turned state's evidence.

The suspects were in custody, but the Mexican authorities had a problem: all they had was a book by an angry ex-wife and four girls who swore they hadn't been kidnapped. ████████ even ran away from home and told a Mexican paper that she was still in love with ████████. Soon, though, other girls began coming forward. A former Guerrero state beauty queen told the police that ████████ had raped her in front of the other girls. A girl who had joined ████████ circle after participating in a ████ look-alike contest in Santiago, Chile, said that when she refused to have sex with ████████, he whipped her with a utility cord and tore off her clothes. She and her sister, who had also joined the group, eventually escaped, she said, and made their way back to Chile.

Finally, ████████ had a change of heart. She filed charges of her own and in 2001 released ████████ a book that portrays ████████ as a violent cult overlord. "Sex and punishment took place daily," ████ writes. "That was our way of life." For three years she often had group sex with ████████ and two other girls, she claims, and when she became pregnant, ████████ demanded she abandon her baby "for the good of the group."

████ also had a baby by ████████, ████ writes, but the infant girl choked to death on vomit when she was a 1-month-old in Brazil. (████ admitted that a child of hers died in Brazil, but she would not identify the father. Her lawyers, however, have said that it was ████████ [*Antonio]. The loss devastated ████, according to ████████ account, but that's not the face the star showed the public when her run finally ended. In news photos, she can be seen smiling and blowing kisses from the back of a squad car.

From her seat by the hospital window, ████ scornfully dismissed the protegees who have turned against her. The girls were coerced by imprisonment, she argued, or contradicted themselves, or were cashing in: "I'm sorry, but I know that a person who has been abused doesn't go and tell her story in front of the cameras like that, with a lack of shame."

But if she tried to prove that in a Mexican court, ███ claimed, her life would be in danger. She didn't leave Mexico as a fugitive, she explained, but as an insider with dangerous information about the entertainment industry. Network executives and their political cronies knew she would expose their corruption, she said, so they had initiated this smear campaign.

"Do you know what would happen to me if I went back to Mexico?" she asked. "Activists are killed in Mexico. That's why I hang on here with my fingernails. If I go back and speak up, I could be found dead in my cell, and what would they say? 'She committed suicide.' Who would investigate it? Who would report on it? Nobody, because those are the same people who fear what I have to say." Because she has been a victim of power in both Mexico and Brazil, ███ lawyers have insisted she should be released on human rights grounds and granted political asylum.

███, however, never said anything about corruption or conspiracies until after her arrest. And if she were truly in danger, why did she take five teenagers on the run with her? Possible corruption in the entertainment world also does not explain ███ repeated problems with adolescent girls. As for that, ███ said, it's really a matter of context. "In the United States, a minor is a minor, and that's a crime," she explained. "In Mexico, if the minor is over 12 or 14, it's not a violation, and you can't say anything."

It was getting dark, and ███ had grown tired. She asked if I would like to hear a song she wrote in prison. I was surprised to find that she has a beautiful, delicate voice.

A pattern of applause came from the door where pregnant

mothers from other rooms were gathering and the two police officers were softly clapping. Her eyes glistening, ███ dedicated the next song to all their future babies.

One week later, on Feb. 18, ████████████████ was born. The Brazilian police seized the placenta, and 75 prison guards and police officers offered their DNA for paternity testing. But one volunteered sample cleared them all, including ████: the father, investigators say, is ███████████ [*Antonio].

The police now believe that ████ bribed guards for time alone with ██████ in an attorney-client conference room. ██████ lawyers have demanded independent DNA tests, claiming that the government doctored the results to hide its complicity in ████ rape. But perhaps ████ already hinted at the truth herself, in her song about lifting the mountains from a dear friend's shoulders. Because ██████████ was born on Brazilian soil, ███████ ██████ may also be the parent of a Brazilian child. If so, he now has as strong a claim to freedom as ████.

Christopher McDougall is a writer at large for Philadelphia magazine.

A version of this article appears in print on April 6, 2002 of the National edition with the headline: Slick Transit ██████.

I believe that after reading this, we can get an even better sense of what all of this has been about. This is why so many times, when people know just a little about what happened, the comments tend to be about how Mexico has no memory. Yet this is not only something we see in Mexico; obviously, this happens around the world, both with people who hold a public position of power and behind closed doors, in relationships nobody can see. The narratives we are exposed to by people who manipulate situations, knowing they can get away with them, are frightening.

I've often heard how "power corrupts," and have analyzed on several occasions if that is a general truth or if it has to do with the darkness of some of the people who reach a position of power. Maybe it has to do with a sense of entitlement, of getting away with different things for enough time, that the conclusion is that we can do as we please, no matter how many lives are harmed along the way. The thing is, dear readers, we are all accountable at the end of the day; it doesn't matter if we believe otherwise, and the idea that some lives matter more than others is one of the root problems of our past and our present. Every single life matters. We hold an intrinsic value just for existing, and nobody should ever be treated as merchandise. People are not for sale. Lives are not for sale. No amount of money, fame, or power is a reason to believe anybody owes us anything.

Another brief article I came across is one that talks about Jane. Jane has also taken it upon herself to have her story told through her own voice in a podcast.

Ex-█████ Backup Singer Held for Trial in Rape

L.A. TIMES ARCHIVES

APRIL 8, 2003 12 AM PT

FROM TIMES WIRE REPORTS

The former backup singer of imprisoned Mexican pop idol █████████████ was ordered held for trial in Mexico on charges of aggravated rape, kidnapping and corruption of minors.

█████████████████████, known as ███████████, will be transferred to the women's area of a maximum-security prison where ████ also is being held.

████████ was extradited last week from Brazil, where she had been imprisoned since January 2000 along with ████ and ████ manager, █████████████. Prosecutors say the three recruited teenage girls for live-in musical training and forced them to have sex with █████████.

How is it that all of this is documented and Karola's story, as well as the stories of so many other victims, are considered lies? In one of the interviews done with Antonio, Laura, and Jane while they were in jail in Brazil, Antonio started to read out loud the letter Karola sent him as a means to justify that all of the girls actually loved him and desired him. I have to add, again, that in the case of Karola, she was so coerced, manipulated, and terrified, that she wrote this letter replying to a letter Antonio sent her as a means to keep the peace because she feared for her life and for her son's life.

The transcript of the interview goes like this:[80]

*After Antonio reads a part of the letter.

Interviewer, "And you believed this?"

Antonio, "Yes."

Interviewer, "From all of them?"

Antonio, "Yes."

Interviewer, "You have told me about a TV station, how they plotted all of this. Later, it was the government, then all the corruption followed. Antonio, let me also ask you, did a TV station make you father seven children with seven different women and have them say that you hit them, mistreat them, and don't let them leave? Is that also television?"

*At this point, Laura, who had tried to interrupt the interviewer several times while she was asking these questions, finally interrupts and answers on behalf of Antonio. She defends him and, consumed with anger, replies:

Laura, "That's just them displaying this. They're airing some intimacies and putting cream on their tacos because they don't talk about how the father of Paola has two children with a woman, and both sisters, the mother and the aunt, were in the same house, sharing details about how the father was. And that the father was also involved with another woman at his job, with whom he also had children. Right? They don't care about that."

Interviewer, "And does that justify this?"

Laura, "No, it doesn't justify it, but neither does it justify the television network doing what they are doing to us, to me."

Interviewer, "But I don't think a television network said, 'Antonio, you are going to do this, and the girls are going to put legal complaints.'"

Antonio, "Girls no, girls no."

Interviewer, "Alright, young ladies."

*Laura interrupts again:

---

80   Barrón, Lidia, and ReTrO TV. "█████ Realizada Por La Periodista Lidia Barrón En Brasil a ███████ y ████████ • 2001." YouTube, January 16, 2023. https://www.youtube.com/watch?v=KOmrrmPCvzM.

Laura, "Birthed women."

While these types of interviews were circling in the media, Karola kept growing in love and faith. Her beautiful son was growing, and he was healthy; she met a man, experienced the wonderful life event of falling in love, got married, and was blessed with another baby. Her faith continued to grow by the minute, and her relationship with God provided her the opportunity to live gratefully and with hope. Her life had shifted 180 degrees, yet as with every path, nothing was linear. She also continued to live in fear. Fear that something would happen to her family if Laura and Antonio left prison, fear that they would take her son away from her, and fear of being constantly recognized because of the tabloids.

She told me about her first Christmas when she had finally moved away from it all. When we talked about it, I could feel how this experience gave her so much. With her husband at the time, and sons, she moved to Cancun, when it was pretty much just a small town. Her first Christmas was something extraordinary because of lack and abundance, which, when they can coexist, transform the experience into one that is permeated with gratitude. She bought her Christmas tree at a supermarket on Christmas day, when they were the cheapest, and decorated it, together with her young boys, with cotton balls. She remembers this Christmas to the very last detail because she felt safe. Economically, they were tight, but having a home full of love made her the wealthiest woman in the world. Her children were healthy, happy, and, most importantly, they were all free.

Creating a home that provides a sense of peace and safety is not an easy task, particularly when you have been enslaved. It involves so much love, creativity, patience, and connection. We know it goes beyond mere decoration but is more about creation—creating an environment that gives ourselves and our loved ones a feeling of belonging, familiarity, and, of course, emotional security. Our home becomes an extension of ourselves, serving as a stable haven, a sanctuary.

She did this for herself and for her family at a very young age after all that she had experienced. She had her safe haven, with creaking floorboards and unique smells, where her children would run around and play, where she cooked nutritious food after being starved, where she was able to sleep without fearing for her life, creating cherished memories she holds dear in her heart.

She didn't have many skills at the time, or academic studies to get a job, yet she persevered. She put one foot in front of the other every single day, even though she felt lost. Life's meaning wasn't clear, and even with her faith, she experienced many symptoms related to post-traumatic stress, obviously.

I ask you, dear readers, to close your eyes and think of the most difficult moments you have ever endured. Now, think about the time, work, and resources it took to get to the other side. Life is a process for all of us, and overcoming our difficulties is something that doesn't happen out of the blue. We have to do what heals us consistently.... Yet, sometimes, it seems like life itself gets in the way.

For Karola, it wasn't only the economic struggles or healing from years of slavery; it was also a car crash. A crash she was in with Jonathan, where a dear friend of hers lost his life, and where the only words she could utter after the impact were, "God, please save my son." It seemed like even in freedom, life's difficulties kept testing her, but she persevered. I know I have said this before and will probably say it again, but among the most impressive characteristics Karola has is her attitude. I can't really say if it is because of everything she has experienced or in spite of it, but she is an example of love and light.

Karola has dealt with a great amount of death in her short life, both literally and figuratively, and death changes us. If I can share anything about the grief process from a personal point of view, which Karola and I have discussed, it's the following:

1. Grief is *not* linear. It's not linear on the first day, the first month, the first year, or the first decade. It oscillates between acceptance and denial with the swiftness of a butterfly's wings, and all the emotions and stages of grief that are on the spectrum of grays feel anything but gray. Denying what we feel is normal because we don't like the pain. However, denial won't take us out of the pain.

2. Anger hides behind every corner, and it might show up unexpectedly when you realize certain little things, like, for example, that you will never get a phone call from that person again. It is also present constantly, somehow becoming the bodyguard for sadness. Anger is one of the strongest emotions and is part of the pain, but eventually, it reaches its climax and begins its descent

until it dissipates. Both anger toward death and anger toward the one who "left us" transform.

3. We understand many things about our relationships after years of absence, and unfortunately, it's true that we only value what we have until it's gone. We never stop missing them.

4. At the beginning of the grieving process, having a good time, laughing, and enjoying life feels like a betrayal to the one who died. It's not. Having small moments of enjoyment while we go through the pain of grief may be just what keeps us afloat.

5. *There's no rush*. The time it takes for each of us is personal, and there's no "correct" time. In research I did on pathological grief several years ago, it's called this way to label grief that lasts more than two years, and that includes many other factors. It can take many years to feel better, and that's valid and doesn't mean we're doing something wrong or experiencing pathological grief. Let no one pressure us—this has more to do with other's intolerance toward our pain and the difficulties that come with it, as well as the rush and fantasy of returning to normal (by the way, that never happens), than with our individual, natural grieving process. Surrounding ourselves with people who deny our pain or lack the emotional tools to accompany us during this time, leads to irreparable fractures in relationships.

6. Time is our ally, but more than time itself, it's what we do while it passes. Crying, screaming, writing, singing, dancing, going to therapy, praying, talking to our loved ones...whatever works for each of us is valid. Holding back emotions makes them rot and prevents us from moving forward.

7. The fear of our loved ones' death tends to be more present than before, which, despite generating anxiety that can be worked on, also connects us with the vulnerability of absolutely everything, and this can help us value the relationships we have in the present time.

8. We can learn to connect, in the way that comes most naturally to us, with those who are no longer here.

9. Their smell, their voice, the texture of their skin, and the color of their eyes tend to get gradually lost in the corners of our memory.

However, the phrases, the looks, and the gestures remain alive through others, and this is a gift.

10. We can forgive someone who is no longer here without receiving an apology. We can also apologize even without getting a response. The process is personal. We can heal the wounds of relationships without the other person being present, and that frees us both.

Having genuine support through our grieving processes, whether due to the loss of a loved one or the loss of a life we once had, helps us transform our experience. For Karola, the presence of her loved ones and strong support system helped. Having her basic needs met helped. Having opportunities and the possibility of a future with her children helped. Having love in her life helped. She has told me many times that the catalyst in this period of her life, and in every other period, has been having God in her life. Yet, at the beginning stages of her healing journey, the existential vacuum she experienced wanted to take over.

"The Lord will protect and preserve him; He will bless him in the land and refuse to surrender him to the will of his foes" (Psalm 41:2, BSB).

CHAPTER 17:
The Existential Vacuum

I don't know if you have ever heard of Viktor Frankl.... To truly delve into and understand the origins of Viktor Frankl's work, we must consider his historical context. Frankl was born into a Viennese Jewish family in 1905. From a young age, he had a keen interest in psychology and mental health, and his self-taught education included numerous texts on psychoanalysis, which was highly popular among European psychiatrists. He also developed a strong interest in philosophy, which would greatly influence his exploration of existential questions related to the meaning of life.

During his student years, Frankl had many opportunities to become acquainted with pain. He even wanted to specialize in the study and treatment of depression and suicide prevention, offering support services to students experiencing excessive stress throughout the 1930s. Unfortunately, it was his own experience as a prisoner in Nazi concentration camps that truly put his philosophy into practice.

In 1942, Frankl was deported to a ghetto and, from there, to various concentration camps. Most of his family, including his mother, father, first wife, colleagues, and friends, perished in the extermination camps while Frankl endured slave labor conditions until the camp he was in was liberated in 1945.

In his work *Man's Search for Meaning*, Frankl mentions that in life, we do not merely live, but we also survive, and survival involves giving meaning to suffering. Frankl devotes an entire book to the suffering individual, which constitutes the anthropological foundation of logotherapy.[81]

In the face of a lack of meaning in life, when one experiences what Lukas referred to as "value blindness," as well as existential paralysis, a type of neurosis called noogenic neurosis, as coined by Viktor Frankl, is experienced. This neurosis can be understood as a "disease of the spirit," characterized by existential emptiness, a state of tedium, boredom, and frustration of the will to meaning.[82]

---

81   Frankl, Viktor. *El Hombre en Busca de Sentido*. Herder, 1990.
82   Lukas, Elisabeth. *Logoterapia: La Búsqueda de Sentido*. Barcelona: Paidós, 2003.

This attitude is characterized by both nihilism (expecting nothing) and fatalism (believing there is nothing one can do to change the situation), and it involves hopelessness, a lack of important goals, as well as a lack of a life project. Frankl defined the term "existential vacuum" as a loss of interest in life and a lack of initiative and proactivity, which can lead to deep feelings of meaninglessness.

Other characteristics of the existential vacuum include a basic confusion between desire and reality, escapism, sadness/despair, tedium/boredom, anger/aggression, aversion, as well as the abandonment of responsibilities and objective commitments, the unsatisfactory pursuit of experiences, and a general sense of emptiness and suicide. The existential vacuum, contrary to the sense of life that is linked to the realization of values, corresponds to a difficulty and incapacity to perceive the possibility of realizing values in everyday existence; in other words, an axiological blindness.

For Frankl, this lack of meaning in life, the idea that life lacks value, is absurd and organically leads to the frustration of the will to meaning, and it is one of the main causes of depression and suicide. He believed that at least 20 percent of cases diagnosed as major depressive disorder or dysthymia are due to a lack of meaning in life or an existential vacuum.

The existential vacuum is a disorder of a spiritual nature whose origin lies in the spiritual dimension of the person. It is not related to a mental problem; it is etiologically spiritual, a moral conflict, or an existential crisis. According to Frankl, the person is a somato-psychic-spiritual unity, and within this unity, there is a hierarchy, with the spiritual being superior to the psychosomatic.[83]

According to Frankl, the existential vacuum leads to the search for pleasure, success, or any other substitute for meaning in which the person who experiences it escapes from their reality in search of experiences and pleasures unrelated to their way of life and vocation. These would be manifestations of the substitution of the "will to meaning" for the "will to pleasure" and the "will to power." According to Frankl, such will for pleasure or will for power only forms when the will to meaning has been frustrated—when the pleasure principle becomes a neurotic motivation.[84]

Furthermore, Frankl asserts that humans can decide for themselves,

83   Frankl, Viktor E. *La idea psicológica del hombre*. Madrid: Ediciones Rialp, 2003.
84   Frankl, Viktor E. *En el principio era el sentido*. Barcelona: Paidós, 2000.

which is possible thanks to the freedom of personal attitude, which itself is the existential change. He considers the spiritual aspect as "the freedom within man" to the extent that only what can behave freely, regardless of circumstances, is considered a person. It is the freedom to be and the freedom to become something different since existence is within its respective possibility.[85]

For Frankl, human beings primarily seek meaning, which becomes a problem only when it is lost. This can occur in various situations, such as mental or physical illnesses, loneliness, losses, and separations, among others. In any case, the lack of meaning can become a significant problem that may even lead to suicide. The existential vacuum is neither pathological nor pathogenic but rather a spiritual anguish that is by no means a mental illness.[86]

This struggle for meaning can, of course, be frustrated, and this frustration can lead to noogenic neurosis, which others might call spiritual or existential neurosis. Paradoxically, if what one desires is to find meaning, then the lack of it becomes a hole, a void in our lives. Therefore, upon having it, we seek to fill it. When trying to fill existential voids with "things" that, because they provide some satisfaction, are often expected to provide ultimate satisfaction. Consequently, human beings mistakenly seek to fill these voids with pleasure, conformity, conventionality, vicious circles, and even anger. This only leads to a feeling of chronic insufficiency. Neurotic vicious circles are based on what Frankl refers to as anticipatory anxiety: someone may be so afraid of experiencing certain anxiety-related symptoms that having those symptoms becomes inevitable.

Frankl refers to depression, addiction, and aggression as the massive neurotic triad. He mentions research showing a strong relationship between the lack of meaning and behaviors, such as criminality and involvement in drugs. He warns that violence, drug use, and other negative behaviors only convince the "meaning-hungry" individuals that their lives can improve by engaging in such conduct. Analyzing it from the perspective of logotherapy, the characteristics of the existential vacuum are complemented by its symptoms, implying that a person experiencing the vacuum may have sadness, melancholy, anguish, loneliness, depression, alcoholism, drug addiction, conformity, engaging in violent acts

---

85   Frankl, Viktor E. *Ante el Vacío Existencial*. Ed. Herder, Barcelona, 1990.
86   Ídem.

against others or oneself (homicide, suicide, suicide attempts), as well as any self-destructive attitude, and/or activity that generates apathy, demotivation, and even disconnection from society.

Frankl's analyses point to social and cultural elements as responsible for this type of frustration. However, the psychological element suggests that individuals experience this frustration when they turn the means to self-realization and transcendence into ends in themselves to attain happiness. This happens because when the means become an end, it becomes a destructive agent for the individual since the search for meaning is rooted in the transcendence of the person. According to Frankl, a person will only attain these means as an indirect consequence of the search for meaning. Conversely, when they are turned into an end, an object of longing, they move further away.[87]

I don't know if you've ever experienced the call of the void. It is a very intense experience. It's when you are somewhere, very high up, and feel the urge to jump. Even though you are scared and know you won't, you feel a pull. Literally. It's like a hypnotizing pull you have absolutely no control over. Some people feel it, some don't, and most just ignore it.

To address the void might be one of the most crude and difficult things to do. It's the existential emptiness that makes us realize that absolutely nothing will fill the void. The emptiness we all experience at some point, and that doesn't go away, so we are up against it and have to find a way to transform it, which, in my opinion, is one of life's greatest lessons.

The good news, my dear readers, is that precisely through this void or existential vacuum is where we find the will to meaning. For many of us, it is how we find our path in life, in faith, in God. As the beautiful quote often attributed to Robert Frost says, "The only way out is through." Karola experienced this in the most intense manner, which, in turn, gave way to her resilience.

---

87   Fabry, Joseph B. *Pursuit of Meaning*, 1994.

CHAPTER 18:
Resilience

After researching countless authors who talk about resilience for my PhD investigation, I have to say that Edith Grotberg is one of my favorites. She has been investigating resilience since way before it was popular, with The International Resilience Project in 1995.[88] Grotberg defines resilience as a universal capacity that allows a person, group, or community to prevent, minimize, or overcome the damaging effects of adversity. Resilience may transform or make the lives of those who are resilient. The resilient behavior may be in response to adversity in the form of maintenance or normal development despite the adversity or a promoter of growth beyond the present level of functioning. Further, resilience may be promoted not necessarily because of adversity but, indeed, may be developed in anticipation of inevitable adversities.[89]

Her paradigm consists of three components: I have, I am, and I can. "I have" supports around each individual to promote resilience, and its building block is trust. "I am" encourages developing the inner strengths of confidence, self-esteem, and responsibility, with its building blocks being autonomy and identity. "I can" is about the acquisition of interpersonal and problem-solving skills, with its building blocks being initiative and industry.[90]

To me, Grotberg's way of defining and categorizing resilience is beautiful and simple. The I am, I have, I can paradigm is something we can all learn from that doesn't require much. For me, it has become a type of motto that helps me ground myself when I am becoming overwhelmed.

My PhD investigation was about resilience and the meaning of life after human trafficking. I learned so much from the amazing women who took part in the study, and also about resilience and logotherapy and its life values.

---

88   Grotberg, Edith. "A Guide to Promoting Resilience in Children: Strengthening the Human Spirit." La Haya, Holanda: The Internacional Resilence Proyect. Bernard Van Leer Foundation, 1995.

89   Grotberg, Edith. The International Resilience Project: Research and Application, 1998. https://files.eric.ed.gov/fulltext/ED423955.pdf.

90   Grotberg, Edith. Countering Depression with the Five Building Blocks of Resilience , 1999. https://cpor.org/ri/CounteringDepression-5ResilienceBuildingBlocks.pdf.

Viktor Frankl's logotherapy has extraordinary values that I want to share:

1. Values of experience: It refers to what the human being receives from the world, both those experiences of suffering and experiences of personal construction.

2. Values of creation: It refers to how the human being responds to the world, with the intention of being able to provide something to the world. When you experience that you are not only capable of giving something to the world but that you can offer something through your own creations.

3. Attitude values: The ability of a human being to find meaning in suffering; this value is given through the stance that the person takes in the face of pain and how it can generate dignity and integrity, courage and serenity to give new meaning to suffering in order to transform it and strengthen resilience.

The attitude values are those that introduce the "tragic triad," which is made up of the triple challenge that they represent, suffering, guilt, and death, and which puts the human being in contact with the human condition in front of limit-situations.[91]

Going a step further, logotherapy proposes that meaning in life can be discovered in three distinct ways:

- By creating.

- By experiencing something or encountering someone.

- By the attitude that we take toward unavoidable suffering.

I won't try to explain a 300-page thesis in a couple of paragraphs, and I will definitely not bore you to death with the details of the methodology, but I will tell you just a little about some of the findings. For the women who took part in my research, what helped them develop resilience and find meaning in life was strongly linked to the people who believed in them after everything that happened to them.

Their meaning of life was manifested mainly by the motivation that led to the realization of pleasant activities that, in consequence, fostered

---

91   Frankl, Viktor. *Logotherapy and Existential Analysis*. Barcelona: Herder, 1990.

positive bonds, promoting learning and gratitude. In relation to resilience, the participants experienced motivation in the activities they carried out, determination towards the goals that led to independence, and recognition of positive personality attributes and opportunities that fostered the construction of healthy self-esteem.

The participants experienced an existential void and frustration of the will to meaning. They presented sadness, anguish, loneliness, depression, substance abuse, violent acts toward others and themselves, as well as self-destructive activities that generated demotivation and detachment from society.

The meaning of life capacities in the surviving victims of human trafficking who participated in my research were activated mainly through motivation, gratitude, learning, faith, pleasurable activities, altruism, and positive bonds. The impact of the experience itself, as well as the confrontation with the limitations of their own lives, led the participants to recognize what happened to them, accept it, and thus find a way to adopt a stronger attitude.

In other words, doing personal work is important, but so are the positive bonds we make with the people around us. It takes a village, and when you actually think about it, pretty much everything in life does.

The importance of healthy emotional bonds cannot be overstated when it comes to anything in life, but when we are talking about something so impactful like helping human trafficking survivors overcome the profound trauma they have endured, warm, nurturing relationships provide a crucial foundation for healing, restoring trust, and rebuilding a sense of self-worth.

Human trafficking often leaves survivors feeling isolated, broken, and disconnected from others. By nurturing healthy and positive emotional connections, we can create an environment where survivors feel valued, supported, and understood. Genuine connections based on empathy, compassion, and unconditional acceptance play an important part in helping survivors regain their trust in others and rebuild their ability to form meaningful relationships.

A genuine connection approach to support survivors involves creating safe spaces where they can share their experiences where they are believed, without fear of judgment or shame. Active listening, empathy, and validation are also essential components of building these bonds. By truly listening to survivors' stories and acknowledging the pain they have endured, we communicate that their experiences are valid and that they are not alone in their journey.

Family, friends, and chosen support systems play a crucial role in providing healthy emotional bonds. These relationships offer survivors a sense of belonging and that provides a shoulder to lean on, offering reassurance during unimaginable moments of vulnerability. It is a genuine opportunity to rebuild trust in a nurturing environment and develop a supporting network that can be transformative, providing survivors with a stable foundation from which to heal and grow.

In addition to personal relationships, professional support is instrumental in helping survivors form healthy emotional bonds. Therapists, counselors, and support groups specializing in trauma-informed care offer survivors a safe and structured environment to address their emotional needs. These professionals guide survivors through the healing process, helping them develop coping strategies, process their trauma, and rebuild a positive self-image.

Group therapy and support networks provide survivors with opportunities to connect with others who have experienced similar traumas, fostering extremely powerful bonds that offer a sense of understanding, community, and shared strength. This, in turn, paves the way toward gaining validation, learning from each other, and finding solace in knowing that they are not alone in this journey.

Beyond personal relationships, community support is vital in helping survivors overcome trauma. Communities can foster environments that prioritize empathy, compassion, and inclusivity, enabling survivors to feel accepted and supported as they reintegrate into society. Public awareness campaigns, educational initiatives, and community events can help raise awareness about human trafficking, reduce stigma, and encourage community members to become advocates for survivors.

We can be part of this community, even if it is just by having difficult conversations with our loved ones, which, in turn, will have a ripple effect of love and responsibility. Constructing healthy emotional bonds isn't only sunshine and rainbows; it's about the difficulties, too. They are essential for all of us, and for human trafficking survivors, they are an extraordinary resource to heal, overcome trauma, and rebuild their lives.

Whether through personal relationships, professional support, or community involvement, the warmth of these bonds helps survivors reclaim their sense of self-worth, build resilience, and rediscover the power of human connection on their journey towards re-becoming.

When you think about it, healthy emotional bonds help us no matter what it is we are dealing with...even if we aren't dealing with any difficulties at the moment. Having "our people," "our village," and "our support system" is life-changing. Because we are social beings (even those of us who aren't that social), and we need each other. When we have healthy emotional bonds, life is just better.

The relationship that exists between resilience, the meaning of life, and human development is given from an interactive and dynamic perspective of adaptive processes, both those related to emotional management as well as to the social experience. The meaning of life is directly linked to resilience through attitude values. These provide the ability to find meaning in suffering and, in this way, give rise to courage, give a new meaning to it, and transform it. Through resilience, said transformation continues its process, providing the ability to adapt to a new reality and expanding the meaning of life, which reinforces a dynamic, contextual, and systemic perspective of human development.

I have had the opportunity to get to know many human trafficking survivors, and I can genuinely say that if someone encompasses attitude values, it is Karola. Her perspective on life, love, faith, and everyday situations is inspiring. Her bravery in sharing her story for the first time gives us the opportunity to really learn and understand.

In the words of the United Nations, "In the fight to end human trafficking, let survivors lead the way."

CHAPTER 19:
Mexico

At the risk of sounding like Dorothy in *The Wizard of Oz*, there is no place like Mexico. Seriously, its rich cultural heritage that is deeply rooted in ancient civilization, which in turn is reflected in the art, music, traditions, and architecture, is sublime. We have the Mayan ruins of Chichen Itza with the Pyramid of Kukulcan and the Temple of Warriors. We have Teotihuacan, with the Pyramid of the Sun, the Pyramid of the Moon, and the Temple of the Feathered Serpent (Quetzalcoatl). We have El Tajin, a city of ancient Totonac civilization that astonishes anyone with the Pyramid of the Niches; Uxmal, with the Pyramid of the Magician, the Governor's Palace, and the Nunnery Quadrangle; Tulum, with its picturesque setting with the ruins perched on cliffs above the beach...I could go on and on.

The food? Honestly, nothing beats Mexican cuisine...tacos, enchiladas, salsa, guacamole...I just got very hungry. Above everything, the Mexican people are warm and welcoming, know how to treat people kindly and how to throw a good party! The festivals and celebrations are witness to the rich cultural heritage, along with the artistic expression and craftsmanship.... There is no place like Mexico.

The landscapes and beaches? You can't begin to imagine. Along both its Pacific and Caribbean coasts, including jungles, mountains, underwater caves, rocky cliffs, dramatic coastlines, and serene, white sandy beaches. The mangroves, lagoons, and unique coastal dune systems will undoubtedly take anyone's breath away. The crystal-clear turquoise waters, especially in the Caribbean region, the calmness of the seas, and the visibility of the water make anyone feel they are dreaming.

Mexico's beach destinations often combine natural beauty with the cultural richness of coastal towns and cities, such as Tulum, Cancún, Playa del Carmen, and Puerto Vallarta, that offer a blend of stunning beaches, historical sites, and vibrant local traditions, making them appealing to tourists seeking both natural and cultural experiences.

I write the following with so much pain, yet it is also appealing to tourists looking to engage sexually with underage girls and boys. Mexico is broken. Mexico kills its women and is ruled by drug cartels; organized crime is surreal; the poverty, inequality, and lack of opportunities continue the vicious cycles of violence and crime...the corruption and impunity? There are no words in the two languages I am fluent in to describe what that is like in Mexico.

The type of violence exerted against women can be physical, sexual, and/or psychological. Gender violence in Mexico has existed since ancient times, mainly as a response to the culture known as machismo, which permeates a significant portion of this society. This violence was defined in 1993 by the United Nations General Assembly as,

> Any act of violence based on the female sex, which results in or is likely to result in physical, sexual, or psychological harm or suffering to women, as well as threats of such acts, coercion, or arbitrary deprivation of liberty, whether it occurs in public or in private life.

Macho culture refers to a set of beliefs, attitudes, and behaviors associated with traditional masculinity, often emphasizing strength, aggression, dominance, and suppression of emotions. It promotes the idea that men should conform to a rigid and stereotypical notion of what it means to be masculine, which can vary across cultures. In a macho culture, there is often an emphasis on physical prowess and a need to assert dominance over others, including women. It may encourage men to engage in competitive and risky behaviors to prove their manhood. This can lead to a disregard for personal well-being and the well-being of others.

Macho culture can also discourage men from expressing vulnerability, emotions, or seeking help, as these qualities may be seen as signs of weakness. This can contribute to issues such as mental health problems, substance abuse, and difficulties in forming and maintaining meaningful relationships. Over time, there has been a growing recognition of the harmful aspects of macho culture, and efforts have been made to promote healthier and more inclusive forms of masculinity that value empathy, emotional intelligence, and respect for others. Mexico is not there yet.

According to UN News, among the fundamental issues related to human trafficking, gender-based discrimination is a key concern, including socio-economic injustices in the countries of origin of women and girls, gender-biased migration policies, and asylum systems in foreign countries, as well as conflicts and humanitarian emergencies.[92]

Trafficking is considered a gender-based crime closely linked to sexual exploitation, and therefore, states must create favorable conditions to ensure the safety of women and girls. Experts also urge the development of public policies that provide autonomy and equitable access to education and employment for women and girls. They also call for the involvement of women in designing gender-based and human-rights-focused responses to the crime.

On another note, the UN special rapporteur on trafficking in persons, Maria Grazia Giammarinaro, mentions that trafficking primarily affects women and girls and often involves unwanted pregnancies, forced abortions, and sexually transmitted diseases. Consequently, she believes that the participation of women is required in conflict responses and post-conflict scenarios to increase awareness of their vulnerability. Giammarinaro emphasized,

> To prevent trafficking and promote the empowerment of women, it is essential to design and implement assistance and recovery measures for trafficking victims in collaboration with survivors and organizations promoting women's rights.

Lastly, it is considered essential for the Security Council to include trafficking in its agenda on "Women, Peace, and Security," which is based on four principles: conflict prevention, participation, protection, and assistance and recovery.[93]

Knowing what goes on in certain parts of a country or the world might help us gain a little insight. What happens to me, my dear readers, is that this "insight" makes my stomach turn. The way things work is so scary and discouraging, and that is precisely when faith comes in. Because what we see and hear is so terrifying that it is too excruciating to believe that is our present reality and our future.

As shocking as this might be, and considering Mexico is the United

---

92   "La Trata de Mujeres y Niñas Se Extiende Al Ciberespacio Por Medio de Las Redes Sociales." United Nations, November 11, 2020. https://news.un.org/es/story/2020/11/1483922.

93   Idem.

States' neighbor...I'm sure if you are reading this in the US, you are feeling the grass is *not* greener in your neighbor's yard. The US is not out of the woods.

The Polaris Project, a leading organization combating human trafficking, operates the National Human Trafficking Hotline.[94] According to their data from 2021,

> 10,359 situations of human trafficking were reported to the U.S. National Human Trafficking Hotline involving 16,554 individual victims. Shocking as these numbers are, they are likely only a fraction of the actual problem.

Certain populations are particularly vulnerable to human trafficking in the United States. These include runaway and homeless youth, individuals with a history of trauma or abuse, individuals with limited English proficiency, migrants, and LGBTQ+ individuals. Minors are especially vulnerable to trafficking. According to the National Center for Missing and Exploited Children, in 2020, they received reports of over 21,000 endangered runaways, many of whom are at risk of being trafficked.[95]

MYTHS ABOUT HUMAN TRAFFICKING

The Polaris Project explains myths surrounding human trafficking in an extraordinary way worthy of sharing:[96]

- Human trafficking is always or usually a violent crime: This is untrue, for even if we might think that human trafficking often involves kidnapping or physically forcing someone into a situation, the reality is that traffickers usually use psychological means such as tricking (which could be through grooming), manipulation, and/or threats.

- All human trafficking involves sex: Human trafficking is the use of force, fraud, or coercion to get another person to provide

94   "Myths, Facts, and Statistics." Polaris, n.d. https://polarisproject.org/myths-facts-and-statistics/.
95   https://www.missingkids.org/
96   "Myths, Facts, and Statistics." Polaris, n.d. https://polarisproject.org/myths-facts-and-statistics/.

labor or commercial sex. Many experts worldwide believe there are more situations of labor trafficking versus sex trafficking, yet there is more awareness of the latter.

- Traffickers target victims they don't know: Survivors have been trafficked by romantic partners, including spouses, and by family members, including parents.

- Only undocumented foreign nationals get trafficked in the United States: Polaris has worked on thousands of cases of trafficking involving foreign national survivors who are legally living and/or working in the United States, including survivors of both labor and sex trafficking.

- Only women and girls can be victims and survivors of sex trafficking: Men and boys are also victimized by sex traffickers. LGBTQ boys and young men are seen as particularly vulnerable to trafficking.

- Human trafficking only happens in illegal or underground industries: Human trafficking cases have been reported and prosecuted in industries including restaurants, cleaning services, construction, factories, and more.

- Human trafficking involves moving, traveling, or transporting a person across state or national borders: Human trafficking is often confused with human smuggling, which involves illegal border crossings. In fact, the crime of human trafficking does not require any movement whatsoever. Survivors can be recruited and trafficked in their own hometowns, even their own homes.

- If the trafficked person consented to be in their initial situation, then it cannot be human trafficking or against their will because they "knew better": Initial consent to commercial sex or a labor setting prior to acts of force, fraud, or coercion (or if the victim is a minor in a sex trafficking situation) is not relevant to the crime, nor is payment.

- People being trafficked are physically unable to leave their situations/locked in/held against their will: That is sometimes the case. More often, however, people in trafficking situations stay for reasons that are more complicated. Some lack the basic necessities to physically get out—such as transportation or a safe place to live. Some are afraid for their safety. Some have been so effectively manipulated that they do not identify at that point as being under the control of another person.

- Labor trafficking is only or primarily a problem in developing countries: Labor trafficking occurs in the United States and in other developed countries but is reported at lower rates than sex trafficking.

- All commercial sex is human trafficking: All commercial sex involving a minor is legally considered human trafficking. Commercial sex involving an adult is human trafficking if the person providing commercial sex is doing so against his or her will as a result of force, fraud, or coercion.

- People in active trafficking situations always want help getting out: Every trafficking situation is unique, and self-identification as a trafficking victim or survivor happens along a continuum. Fear, isolation, guilt, shame, misplaced loyalty, and expert manipulation are among the many factors that may keep a person from seeking help or identifying as a victim, even if they are, in fact, being actively trafficked.

CHAPTER 20:
2004 – 2005

The year The Boston Red Socks won the World Series for the first time since 1918, the strongest earthquake in forty years originated from the Indian Ocean close to Indonesia, creating tsunami waves that swept across much of the coastlines of Sri Lanka, India, Bangladesh, the Maldives, Burma, Thailand, Malaysia, and Indonesia, where at least 290,000 people were confirmed to have died from South Asia to as far as South Africa. Facebook was launched as a social networking site only open to students from Harvard, and The New England Patriots won Super Bowl XXXVIII. This note came out in the Washington Post,

Mexican Pop Star Freed After Judge Dismisses Charges

By Mary Jordan

September 23, 2004

███████████, the Mexican pop music superstar, was cleared by a judge on charges of kidnapping, rape and corruption of minors and walked free Tuesday after spending nearly five years in prison.

A judge in the state of Chihuahua ruled Tuesday that there was not enough evidence to support the charges against ████ and she walked out of Chihuahua prison late in the day. She was met by cheering fans and told a national television audience that she was ready to resume her singing career.

With her trademark long flowing hair and plunging neckline, ████, 36, beamed to the television cameras and said her forthcoming CD would describe her feelings about being incarcerated. Her recordings have sold millions of copies. She told a TV interviewer Tuesday night that she was ready to "take on the world, like never before."

"She is going to come back stronger," said ███████, 18, a ████ fan club leader who said that the singer's fans from Brazil to Argentina and Mexico are thrilled. "It's terrible that she spent so much time with criminals," he said. But, he added, "because she has been repressed for five years, she will come back like a volcano."

Prosecutors had alleged that ███ and her former boyfriend and manager, ██████████, sexually abused girls after kidnapping them into a traveling entourage.

One of ███ accusers said she joined the group at the age of 12 and was impregnated by ██████.

███ and ████████ were arrested in Brazil in January 2000, after more accusations surfaced about the cult-like captivity of young girls.

███ was extradited to Mexico in December 2002 and was held in Chihuahua until her release. Two of ████ backup singers also were cleared Tuesday of the same charges. ██████ is awaiting trial in Mexico.

A taboo-breaker who raffled her panties at concerts, ████ became a symbol of irreverence, especially after the Catholic Church voiced its disapproval.

Known for crude lyrics, near nudity and appearances as a calendar pinup, she became an icon for poor women who liked her sexy, sassy style.

When her career was interrupted five years ago, one headline read: "From Glory to Hell." But a headline in Mexico on Wednesday said: "From Hell to Glory Again."

██████████, vice president of marketing for ████ recording company, BMG, said ████ had written songs in prison that will soon be put on sale. Promoters said Wednesday that plans for a comeback concert were already underway.

There are still unknown details about ████ having become pregnant while locked up in a Brazil prison, where conjugal visits were not allowed. ████ claimed she was raped, but Brazil officials said DNA tests revealed that ████████ was the father.

In the television interview that was also posted on one of her fan club Websites, ████ said, "I am going to miss my companions" in the prison, where "there are a lot of innocent people and those who make mistakes and deserve a second chance."

After nearly five years in prison, superstar ██████████ says she is ready to resume her career.[97]

The Associated Press wrote about Antonio in 2005.

██████ ex-manager will soon be freed despite conviction

In prison 5 years, he will get out of rest of sentence by paying fine and a fee to his accuser

By OKSANA VOLCHANSKAYA, Associated Press March 23, 2005

CHIHUAHUA, MEXICO—A judge Tuesday sentenced the former manager of pop star ████████ to just under eight years in prison for rape, kidnapping and corruption of minors, but will allow him to go free on time served after paying reparations to his accuser and a small fine.

████████ has been behind bars for five years and Judge ████████ said he can be excused from the remainder of his sentence of seven years and 10 months by paying about $90,200 to his chief accuser, ████████, and her family.

He also will be charged $326 in court fines.

████████ "received this sentence because he had no prior criminal record and was very well-behaved during his time in prison," ████ said. "He's not considered a danger to society."

It took the judge hours to read the more than 300-page case file before announcing the verdict. ██████ listened from inside a metal courtroom cage.

He did not speak to reporters before returning to his cell.

Accuser not present

Despite assurances she would be present, ████ was not in the courtroom for the ██████ verdict.

Jordan, Mary. "Mexican Pop Star Freed after Judge Dismisses Charges." The Washington Post, September 23, 2004. https://www.washingtonpost.com/archive/politics/2004/09/23/mexican-pop-star-freed-after-judge-dismisses-charges/fe8c793a-ad6f-4f74-9402-c514f1783bcb/.

███ gave birth to and later abandoned a baby in Spain in 1998. Forensic tests showed ██████ was the father.

After the discovery of the abandoned baby, police filed charges against ████ and ██████, who vanished but were arrested in Brazil in January 2000.

During the proceedings against him, ████████ testified about having sex with ████, but denied raping her or kidnapping her.[98]

Antonio received a sentence of seven years and ten months in prison. He was released in 2007.

When Karola and I talked about how she felt about this when it happened, she told me that when she heard the news about Laura, which was four years after she was finally free, she didn't fully understand what was happening. Her feelings were somewhat contradictory. On one hand, Karola's heart went out to Laura, who had lost her baby daughter just a little over a month after she was born. Karola figured that after such a horrifying experience and years in jail, maybe something changed in her. On the other hand, she felt frustrated and angry because of the tears and lies that led to severe manipulation portrayed by the media. She remembers the grooming; she remembers how Laura was such an important part of the nightmare lived by so many young girls, and yet, "there was insufficient evidence."

She felt gaslighted by the media and attacked by Laura's fans, who, to this day, are extremely aggressive, even if Karola hasn't said much up until now. Despite all of this, there was a part of her, at a certain point, that believed there must have been a good reason for Laura's release and that, without Antonio, she would leave all the girls alone. She hasn't stopped instilling terror. She sends threatening messages through her fans and bullies and harasses through news outlets, her books, and movies. She continues to talk about the different victims, currently considering herself a victim as well, which honestly, after years of defending Antonio, came as a shock to many.

In an interview held in 2004, after she was out of jail, Laura was

98   Volchanskaya, Oksana. "██████ Ex-Manager Will Soon Be Freed despite Conviction." Chron., March 23, 2005. https://www.chron.com/news/nation-world/article/████-s-ex-manager-will-soon-be-freed-despite-1923912.php.

questioned about her part in everything that happened.[99] It is an interview worth watching, over an hour long, and I have extracted and transcribed certain parts I consider pertinent as a demonstration of what Karola and all of the other victims were seeing in the mass media about what had happened to them. Mind you, I must admit that there are parts of this interview when Laura talks about what happened to her baby daughter where I found myself with tears in my eyes and feeling compassion toward her. Curiously, though, this compassion fled rapidly due to everything else she said.

Statement after describing what happened to her daughter (minutes 15:30–16:46),

"The bandage fell from my eyes, and I am happy to be alive. Because disguised as friends, as sisters, they were people who envied what I had, what I wore, how I was wanted, what I did, what I wanted, and in many cases, they wanted to be me. I mean, they didn't want to just look like me; they wanted to be me and have what I had. I was very naive. I mean, I didn't realize it, or at a certain point, I took it as flattery."

Interviewer, "That is respect to them, and to him? When did your love for him end?"

Laura, "At that moment." (When she found out what had really happened to her daughter.)

[...]

Interviewer, "There are some very serious accusations...absolved—absolved. But one knows, and one knows oneself; we know our own story, we know our past, we lived it, and we carry it with us all the time. Look, I have a son...." The interviewer proceeded to talk about her thirteen-year-old son and then told Laura, "There were girls that age that arrived with you" (implying the "academy"), and then asked Laura, "You now have a son, would you like something like that to happen to him?"

To which she replied, "Absolutely never."

[...]

Interviewer, "There were moments where you all lived under the same roof..."

Laura, "That was much later."

99   "██████ Con Adela Micha (2004)." YouTube, October 15, 2021. https://www.youtube.com/watch?v=LMFzKSoNfos.

Interviewer, "Yet it is absolutely impossible for you to tell me that you were not aware of what was happening."

Laura, "But that was later, that was much later, we are that talking in '94, '95, '96, '97...'96, '96, I was working nonstop."

Interviewer, "So, when they were teenagers, you didn't realize this was happening, and when they were older is when you started to realize that there were 'situations.'"

Laura, "It is very relative to say teenagers because not all of them were teenagers."

Interviewer, "Well, some of them were."

Laura, "Some of them were."

Interviewer, "Anyway, you no longer have to prove anything."

Laura, "No, no, no."

Interviewer, "In legal and judicial terms, and besides, I am nobody to judge."

Laura, "No, but in moral terms."

Interviewer, "Yes. But you weren't blind; there comes a time when one must assume the responsibility of our actions."

Laura, "But I don't blame anybody. I don't blame anybody. Anybody."

Interviewer, "Exactly, so tell us, tell me, what happened to you. I'm not asking you to blame anybody; I agree with you, especially at thirty-six years old; one has to assume the consequences of our actions."

Laura, (snapping her fingers) "At thirty-six and at fifteen, and at eighteen, and at any...at nine-years-old, one must learn to assume the consequence of the action one has done, to assume responsibility."

Interviewer, "What was your responsibility in everything that happened? After all this time, what part are you responsible for?"

Laura, "Maybe it was making it too easy for them, the fact that I wasn't interested in material things and that there was a small gold mine, a fortune, a hen laying golden eggs, and letting anyone get them, I think that is what I did wrong. At that moment, I cared very much for all of them and wanted these people to be what I had imagined that they were. Because I know that they are against me, they could have never felt hatred, maybe envy, because thanks to me, they were fed and continue to be fed. I hope they stop being fed thanks to me because it's nice to make a living with one's own hard work and not through the venom that is coming out of their tongues. I am not going to give names. I don't care. I am only interested in being left alone, for them to dedicate their lives to their own things, for them to stop chasing the cameras that are actually looking at my work. They show up wanting to be in the spotlight. You know what? Just get to work, work. If you can't sing, if you can't compose, it's not my fault. God must have given you some type of gift; look for it, find it, and use it because God doesn't leave anyone empty-handed" (minutes 47:36–52:11).

This, dear reader, is revictimization at its finest. And so many questions arose inside me. Supposing—just supposing—she did not have absolutely any idea before '96 of what was happening to so many young women.... She did know what happened from 1996 onward, and that is when Karola arrived.

The interview ended with this statement,

Interviewer, "After 1700 days in prison, she went to the cathedral for mass, giving glory to God in the highest, placing herself at the feet of an image, an act that some relate to the biblical figure of Mary Magdalene. She herself, upon leaving prison, repeated the phrase, 'Let he who is without sin cast the first stone.' And she was captured crying with arms outstretched, saying, 'Glory to God in the highest.' An attitude more typical of priests than of laypeople, but one she transformed into a moment of ecstasy, a mystical and religious experience. Because ████████████████, beyond faith, wanted to be seen with an image of humility, forgiveness, reunion, and even generosity. To fulfill her tithe, she deposited a very personal value, her own ring."

Karola remembers the first time she saw posters of Laura's concerts in Cancun; it frightened her to her core to know they were in the same city.

With respect to when Antonio was released, we talked about that for a really long time. She has blocked that moment of her life, she doesn't really remember it at all. What she does remember is the sense of profound helplessness, impotence, and impunity.

What was extremely helpful to her at that time in her life was living away from it all and having a strong support system. She told me how that felt divinely guided because it gave her the opportunity to contemplate everything outside of the mass chaos, beyond the generalized observer. It was a blessing for her to be in a kind of meditation and communion, finding peace that cleared and organized her thoughts, allowing her to distinguish the real from the unfounded, the thoughts of love from those of fear. She had the chance to feel hatred, cry in solitude, laugh and dance, meet people of faith and those with opposing beliefs, and find her center in an environment without rules or structure.

She had the opportunity to repair her relationship with the Pacific Ocean in the Caribbean Sea in a reunion of sorts that transcended the physical. It was a soul-deep encounter with a force that had been a silent witness to her pain, reminding her of the immense power that lies hidden beneath the surface. She experienced a return to a primal state, a communion, a silent reconciliation to the very essence of her existence.

Her experiences during those years weren't what everyone thought they should be, but they were what worked for her. She delved deeper into her relationship with God and understood, at a soul level, that God accepted her without judgment, without needing to be something that was impossible for her to be. She experienced freedom.

"Let the words of my mouth and the meditation of my heart be acceptable in your sight, O LORD, my rock and my redeemer" (Psalm 19:14, ESV).

CHAPTER 21:
Growth

Growth is painful on any given day. I know I should have probably sugarcoated it a little more, sorry. We have seen it within ourselves and even with our own bodies. It doesn't happen to everybody, but I sure remember growing pains as a child. Even if there is no particular data showing growing pains actually happen, they exist. Growth requires so much from us, and that is even considering if our paths are not torn to shreds.

Growing is sometimes so painful that it feels like we are actually breaking. Our bodies change and stretch, just as our thoughts and emotions. We go through several challenging adjustments during our lifetime, and there are times when all we can do is give in and trust the process.

We see it in nature. Plants need to push through the soil to reach the sun, and our personal growth often involves pushing through the most difficult of moments to reach a better place. For Karola, the process of growth, some years after she had been enslaved, was not easy but did lead to increased strength, understanding, and a deeper connection with herself and with God. Yet, embarking on the journey of growth and healing was a very challenging path. She read many books, prayed, and worked so hard to feel like herself again. The thing was, she didn't really know who she was. She was enslaved at such a young age that some of her most formative years were lost in the grueling, traumatic experiences she had, and that takes a toll no matter what things may look like on the outside.

Navigating the aftermath of such trauma brought up all of the emotions, ranging from pain and sorrow to hope and even fleeting moments of happiness. It was never a straight line, more of ebbs and flows, during a period where self-care and self-kindness continued to grow through the confusion. She knew what had happened to her, to her sisters, and to many other young women, but she wasn't yet able to understand it. She was free, but so were Laura and Antonio, and there were many times that nothing made much sense.

The research conducted by Schultz, Canning, and Eveleigh (2020), "Post Traumatic Stress, Posttraumatic Growth, and Religious Coping in Individuals Exiting Sex Trafficking," published in the Journal of Human

Trafficking, includes the terms "posttraumatic growth" and "religious coping" in their investigation with victims of human trafficking in the context of sexual exploitation. They studied the connections between posttraumatic stress, traumatic events, posttraumatic growth, and religious coping. They found that a higher level of religious coping is associated with greater posttraumatic growth, suggesting that it can be of great assistance in the transformation of victims. They also consider that the suffering arising from this terrible experience can paradoxically foster a process of transformation and the use of adaptive strategies.[100]

Similar to how a tree's roots provide stability, Karola's connection to God continued to anchor her and infuse her journey with purpose. Who she once was was gone, and she was beginning to become who she is today. Gradually, she began to uncover a deeper sense of purpose, an expanded capacity for empathy and insight, and a profound sense of serenity that embraced her throughout her path.

It began as a gentle, unfolding journey where she started to expand, learn, and blossom more and more over time. It was slow and steady, with its ups and downs, as she navigated through the darkness that was left by everything that happened. She was focused on raising her boys, learning new skills, and becoming independent. She was slowly discovering parts of her she didn't know existed and had the courage and faith to let go of parts of her that no longer served her. Each experience contributes to a more intricate and enriched young woman.

---

100 Schultz, Tammy, Canning, Sally Schwer, Eveleigh, Elisha. "Posttraumatic Stress, Posttraumatic Growth, and Religious Coping in Individuals Exiting Sex Trafficking, Journal of Human Trafficking," 2020.

CHAPTER 22:
2007

While the global financial crisis started to unfold, Apple released the first generation iPhone, some of us were watching *Grey's Anatomy*, contemplating a career in medicine, J. K. Rowling finished the seventh and last *Harry Potter* novel, British adventurer Jason Lewis completed the first "human-powered circumnavigation of the globe," and Queen Elizabeth II became the oldest-ever monarch of the United Kingdom, Mexico published its first anti-trafficking law in the Official Gazette (*Diario Oficial de la Federación*).

A person who changed the fight against human trafficking in Mexico is Rosi Orozco; thanks to her, for the first time in Mexico, there was a Commission for Human Trafficking. Rosi was the main driver of the Law Initiative to Prevent, Punish, and Eradicate the Offenses of Trafficking in Persons and to Protect and Assist the Victims of These Crimes. This initiative subsequently became a law in Mexico.

In 2008, the attorney general's office created the *Fiscalía Especial para los Delitos de Violencia Contra Las Mujeres y Trata de Personas* (FEMVITRA), a special prosecutor's team designated to work on crimes against women and human trafficking and whose members have received training from international outfits specializing in these matters. President at the time, Felipe Calderón, passed a new law making femicide a crime punishable by up to sixty years in jail. Some radio ad campaigns were launched at a national level to focus on prevention.[101]

These were important steps toward addressing the human trafficking problem but have not been enough to put a dent in human exploitation.

Until that time, Karola had not understood that what had happened to her was human trafficking. This concept was new to her; the experience of it, however, unfortunately not. She had grown personally and spiritually, but to actually understand what had happened to her allowed her to begin a process of transformation.

Being able to label what happens to us gives us the tools to be able to

---

101   Shahani, Arjan. "Human Trafficking in Mexico." Americas Quarterly, June 14, 2013. https://americasquarterly.org/blog/human-trafficking-in-mexico/.

transform what we have lived, and we often confuse growth and transformation. Transformation is like the metamorphosis of a caterpillar into a butterfly. It's a profound change, a rebirth of the spirit. This journey involves embracing the unknown, shedding old layers, and allowing the wings of the soul to unfurl. Through transformation, Karola did not just rewrite chapters of her story; she created an entirely new narrative that radiates the radiant light of her true essence.

Her sons were continuing to grow healthy and happy with the unconditional love and support of their mother. Every single day, she prayed, thanking God for their lives, for their health, and for their freedom. She continued to strive and learn, with some extremely difficult days and others that seemed like they were out of a fairy tale.

Understanding what had happened to her was the beginning of her journey down two paths—growth and transformation. Growth with its gradual progress, and transformation with its radical renewal. Each step she took from that moment on was stronger. She was no longer a victim; she was now a survivor.

"When I am afraid, I put my trust in you" (Psalm 56:3, NIV).

CHAPTER 23:
Finding Our Path

Life is dynamic, and so is our identity, what success looks like, our failures, and, of course, our beliefs. Working on ourselves is dynamic as well, yet to me, personal work is like food. I like the words "personal work" instead of self-help or personal development, just because of the literal aspect of it. It's personal, and it's work we do with and for ourselves. We all eat different foods at different times. Some people have cholesterol problems at a certain time in life and cannot eat certain foods; others are vegetarians, and some people simply hate fruit. That doesn't mean that someone is right and someone is wrong. It means that we are all different, and so are our needs. However, regardless of our tastes, preferences, or health situation, we have to eat every day. The same is true for personal work; it is our food that provides us with what we need to be strong and healthy, and there, right there, lies the power of personal work.

It is feeding ourselves, in this case, the emotional nutrients we need at different times in our lives to be mentally and emotionally healthier. Mental health, fortunately, is already a much more talked about topic and taken seriously. Our emotional health is just as important as our physical health, and they go hand in hand.

Finding our path is not a one-size-fits-all situation; it is not a cookie recipe, and it is not universal. It is individual, ever-changing, and full of surprises that constantly generate shifts within the chaos. It's about learning and practicing flexibility, learning through our mistakes, and deciding what is best for us at any given moment. It's about allowing our brains to rewire, about doing the personal work that is required to be able to confidently and successfully put one foot in front of the other. It is about learning and acquiring new tools that are helpful, about finding ways to slow down without allowing self-sabotage to take the wheel. It is about developing the serenity to accept the things we cannot change, working towards developing our courage to be able to change the things we can, and learning enough from our mistakes to acquire the wisdom to know the difference.

We are all different, and our paths in life are, too. They are unique regarding the time it takes, the medical help, the spiritual help, the psychological help, our genetics, our family environment, our support system, our living situation, our access to resources, our trauma history, our ability to ask for help, our ability to receive help, our ability to accept our difficulties, to learn from ourselves, to learn from situations, and to know no two situations are the same.

Some people believe that faith and psychology don't mix. I believe otherwise, and so does Karola. Our first conversation had moments of discussing different psychological techniques, and in all honesty, although many people are still against therapy, or believe therapy is only for those who are "crazy," psychology is a tool, and honestly, we can use as many tools as we can get at this point. When we have a stomach infection, we need the care of a professional. When dealing with difficulties regarding our mental and emotional experiences, mental health professionals can guide us in a healing process or in a process to better understand ourselves in order to overcome different situations.

Karola has told me on several occasions how different psychological tools have been extremely helpful to her healing process. How there were moments in her life shortly after she was rescued when she felt extremely dirty. Nothing she tried would help. She has told me how, so many years later, the most impactful abuse was sexual abuse; she defines it as the type of abuse that violates your core. The forced labor and the beatings were easier to get over, but the sexual abuse was not. Through a particular exercise she found in a book, she was able to work on this particular issue, and she has had different psychological support throughout the years to help her continue to transform her pain.

Faith and psychology can collaborate and intersect in various ways. While faith is often associated with matters of spirituality, beliefs, and religious practices, psychology focuses on understanding human behavior, cognition, emotions, and mental processes. There are different ways this collaboration occurs, like the integration of spiritual beliefs by psychologists who have an understanding of and respect for diverse faith traditions can incorporate clients' spiritual beliefs and practices into therapy. This integration can provide a holistic approach to mental health and address the spiritual dimensions of a person's well-being. Positive psychology focuses on promoting well-being, resilience, and flourishing. Faith and spirituality can be sources of strength, hope, and resilience for individuals. Psychologists can explore and incorporate positive aspects of faith, such as gratitude, forgiveness, and compassion, to enhance psychological well-being.

Some professionals specialize in pastoral counseling or counseling within religious settings, combining psychological theories and techniques with spiritual guidance to provide support and guidance to individuals seeking help within their faith communities. Many faith communities offer support groups for individuals dealing with specific challenges such as addiction, grief, or mental health issues. These groups provide a supportive environment where individuals can find understanding, community, and spiritual guidance alongside psychological support.

Psychology explores questions of meaning, purpose, and existential concerns. Faith traditions often offer frameworks and teachings that address these existential questions. Psychologists can draw on these perspectives to help clients find meaning, cope with existential anxiety, and navigate life transitions.

It is important to remember that the collaboration between faith and psychology should respect individual beliefs, be sensitive to cultural diversity, and uphold ethical guidelines. The integration of faith and psychology can provide individuals with a comprehensive approach to well-being, addressing both the psychological and spiritual dimensions of their lives.

CHAPTER 24:
Love

Love has the transformative power to change the world in profound ways. It encourages empathy and compassion towards others, encouraging us to take action to alleviate their suffering. It inspires us to understand and connect with people who are completely different from us, fostering a more inclusive and empathetic society. Karola has told me how love saved her. How the love she felt for her son was what got her through. How even through the largest difficulties she was able to see and feel God's protection.

I believe that feeling love is one of the most extraordinary feelings we can experience. It encompasses everything. When you think about it, we feel the different emotions in our body. Although we are all different, what I have encountered with the different people I have worked with therapeutically is that fear is usually felt in the stomach or chest, anger is felt in the stomach, hands, and throat, sadness is usually felt in the throat and eyes...and love? Love is felt in the entire body.

Love motivates us to perform acts of kindness. Whether it's a small gesture like helping someone in need or engaging in larger-scale charitable endeavors, love prompts us to extend a helping hand. These acts of kindness create a ripple effect, inspiring others to do the same and creating a positive impact in the world. It forms the foundation of strong, nurturing relationships. Healthy relationships based on love, respect, and understanding contribute to personal growth, happiness, and a sense of belonging.

Love also promotes forgiveness, reconciliation, and understanding, allowing conflicts to be resolved peacefully. Love encourages dialogue, empathy, and compromise, which can lead to the resolution of disputes and the establishment of harmonious coexistence. It also drives the fight for social justice and equality. When we truly love our fellow human beings, we recognize the inherent worth and dignity of every single individual. It is a driving force that motivates us to work towards creating a more equitable society where everyone has equal rights and opportunities.

I am personally an imperfect environmentalist, and even love has a role in this. When we genuinely care for something, we strive to protect and preserve it for future generations. In essence, love changes our world by fostering kindness, compassion, understanding, empathy, and equality.

Karola has mentioned to me many times how her love for her sons is what got her through everything. How the birth of her first son connected her to the most profound part of her soul and allowed her to expand her heart. During the many, many times Karola and I discussed the power of love, I became extremely inspired by her take on the subject. Something that allowed me to get to know her even better, and I'm sure you'll feel the same way, is her favorite song. It is originally in Spanish, so this is the best translation I could master. I hope you enjoy it,

When I think about your love
And your faithfulness
I can't do anything else
But bow down and worship

When I think about what I have been
And how far you have brought me
I am amazed by you
I don't want to settle
I have tasted it, and I want more...

I want to fall more in love with you
Teach me to love you and to live
According to your justice and truth
With my life, I want to worship

Everything I have and everything I am
Everything I have been, I give it to you
May my life be for you
Like perfume at your feet

When I think about your cross
And everything you have given
Your blood for me
To erase my sin
When I think about your hand
How far we have come
Because of your faithfulness

I don't want to settle.
I have tasted it, and I want more
I don't want to settle.
I have tasted it, and I want more

I want to fall more in love with you
Teach me to love you and to live
According to your justice and truth
With my life, I want to worship
Everything I have and everything I am
Everything I have been, I give it to you
May my life be for you
Like perfume at your feet.

Through love and faith, Karola has forgiven. She knows she is loved and accepted by God, and she accepts this with her entire being. Her faith and love have had the most profound impact on her life, providing her with the strength, hope, and sense of purpose she now has in the core of her being. She has learned to transcend the circumstances, knowing she is not or has ever been alone.

Through love and faith, Karola wants to share her story to help others. Through love and faith, Karola brought up her two sons, who are wonderful young men. Through love and faith, Karola is now an activist against human trafficking.

CHAPTER 25:
Finding Peace

Peace, although a universal concept and goal, is complex. It's a struggle. I find we can somehow relate it to the concept of happiness. With both, we have to understand that, more than a goal to be reached, it is a state of mind to be experienced. A state of mind that requires practice, strength, and war. Just as pure happiness cannot be experienced without the experience of sadness, peace cannot be experienced if we have not gone through war. And we are constantly at war within ourselves, hence the complexity. It is our responsibility to ourselves to choose peace, to nurture it daily, and to be aware that it is up to us; no one else can do that for us. Yet, the precipitating factors that surround our lives both internally and externally make this a daily challenge.

Internally, there is doubt and faith. There is hate and love. There is revenge and forgiveness. Externally, there is famine and abundance. There is slavery and freedom. There is selfishness and kindness; therefore, there are options. And as human beings, we always have a choice.

We can't choose all the thoughts we think, but we can work tirelessly and practice to learn and relearn how to choose the thoughts we allow to stay—and if depression is taking over, at least we can identify its thoughts as separate from our own. We have to at least be aware because if we are, it is easier to choose how to respond instead of just reacting. We can choose, even if it is excruciatingly painful and exhausting.

Every single day, we get to choose, and just like with absolutely everything else, once we wire or rewire our brains to do something consistently, it becomes easier.

Peace looks different for all of us, but we have to be aware of what we are allowing and nurturing within us; we owe ourselves that much. There will be easier days, and there will be harder days, but it *is* up to you and me to make this shift internally so that we can all, as a whole, experience it externally. I truly believe that what we experience externally collectively is only a reflection of what is going on internally collectively.

Yet, to fully experience peace, there must be freedom; it is somewhat of a prerequisite. We need to have the autonomy to make choices, express ourselves, and pursue our aspirations because the absence of freedom, such as living under any type of oppression, tyranny, or systemic injustice, will inevitably lead to conflict and violation of human rights, making peace elusive. Freedom and peace are interconnected and mutually reinforcing. Achieving and sustaining peace requires safeguarding and promoting freedom, while the exercise of freedom contributes to the maintenance of peace. To be part of the solution, we have to learn and re-learn to respect diverse perspectives, foster tolerance, and promote nonviolent means of conflict resolution, for peace and freedom also create a positive cycle. When we feel safe, respected, and secure, we are most likely to contribute positively to society, engage in peaceful coexistence, and participate actively and lovingly in social, political, and economic life.

Peace and freedom are interconnected and mutually reinforcing. To find peace and experience it, we need to live in freedom, having the ability to exercise our basic human rights, make choices, and pursue our aspirations without undue restrictions or coercion. Living in freedom means having the liberty to live a life of one's choosing, in accordance with one's values and aspirations, while respecting the rights and freedoms of others. It is a fundamental aspect of human dignity and a cornerstone of a just and democratic society. It also entails the enjoyment of fundamental human rights, such as the right to life, liberty, and security of person; freedom of speech, expression, and assembly; and freedom from discrimination and oppression. It involves being treated with dignity and equality.

CHAPTER 26:
Time is the Greatest Storyteller

Over two decades have come and gone since Karola's first audition for an inexistent soap opera, the coercion, the manipulation, the forced labor, the sexual abuse, the psychological abuse, the torture, and the slavery. Although healing and growth are intricate processes that require personal kindness and patience, sometimes, giving this to ourselves is an even bigger challenge than the challenges themselves.

Time, on the other hand, is unburdened by impatience; it reveals truths at its own pace, giving us the opportunity to uncover the profound lessons hidden beneath the surface at our own individual rhythm. As life itself continues to unfold, we can experience how the ordinary moments, in retrospect, were actually extraordinary. There is a reason "hindsight is 20–20," and it has a lot to do with being able to perceive the connections and patterns that lead us to where we are today. It allows us to understand who we are, where we came from, and where we are headed. Time is the invisible thread that binds us to the past, the present, and the future, an endless continuum of experiences that enrich our journey even when we might feel otherwise. Time is the storyteller of all stories.

In the early chapters of Karola's life, when she was constantly struggling with the inner demons born from the difficulties she endured at such an early age, she encountered Christianity, a transformative path that guided her from the darkness to the light. Her spirit, weighed down by the burdens of shame and guilt, was transformed through the teachings of Christianity, for her, a beacon of hope that promised forgiveness, redemption, and a profound opportunity for renewal. As she immersed herself in the teachings of Christ, the words of compassion and unconditional love resonated with her soul, reviving parts she had thought had disappeared. Through the stories of redemption and grace, she was able to see a reflection of her own struggles and where her experiences became enveloped in a newfound understanding, a realization that her worth was not determined by what had happened to her but by the love that embraced her.

During her journey of self-discovery, guided by the principles of Christianity, her interactions with the people around her were transformed, and I can honestly say that spending time with Karola is a wonderful experience for anyone who has the opportunity. Her faith, inner peace, clarity, and hope make the people around her believe even when they are skeptical. The teachings of Christ ignited a fire within her that propelled her to extend a helping hand to those who need it, offer solace to the suffering, and stand up for justice and righteousness.

As time went on, her transformation started to become evident to the people around her. The light that radiated from within seemed to illuminate her path, casting aside the shadows that had once clouded her spirit. She became a source of inspiration, her journey a testament to the power of faith to heal, renew, and uplift. It is through her commitment to her faith that she has found the strength to confront her past, make amends, and continue shining toward the future. She has channeled her experiences into a force for good, using her story to help anyone she can, guiding her toward a life of compassion, purpose, and unwavering faith, becoming a living testament to the power of faith to heal, shape, and elevate the human spirit.

Her faith also helped her while she was raising her two boys. When her youngest was still a boy, she divorced his father, and although they have a good relationship, raising two boys on her own has been quite a journey. A journey filled with never-ending energy as she navigated the exhilarating highs and heartbreaking lows of nurturing and raising these young souls to become good men. She became their compass, helping them navigate life with courage, compassion, faith, and a sense of purpose.

Despite not having a formal education for two decades, she did not waver and consistently and tirelessly strived to create a world of opportunity for her boys. She sought employment doing anything and everything she could, in the early morning hours and burning the midnight oil, embracing every single opportunity that came her way. Her love for her boys, as well as her faith, became the beacon that guided her relentlessly, propelling her toward every single new day.

Even without external stability, she created a world of comfort for her sons. Their needs were her guiding post, and every sacrifice she ever made was worth it.

She has been a fortress of tenderness and strength, nurturing her sons' bodies and souls and planting seeds of faith, hope, and resilience. Her efforts bore fruit, as the boys have blossomed into extraordinary young men. Their journey was not only one of survival; it was one of evolution, a blend of play and reflection. From the days she would sit and build towers with toy blocks and chase fireflies to the difficult conversations, Karola became their mentor, gently steering them toward the right path. She worked hard to foster their independence and provide a safety net to help them build the confidence to chase their dreams while always being there to catch them when they stumbled.

She has had the privilege of watching her sons grow and witnessing them through it all, always being a constant source of love and support, reminding them consistently they are cherished and valued. She focused on teaching them empathy, kindness, and respect, for she knew she was not only shaping their future but also contributing to the future of society. She made it her mission to raise her boys to become good, respectful men, instilling values that transcend gender stereotypes and demonstrating the significance of strength and resilience. Her mothering has been about fostering open dialogue, always encouraging her sons to express their thoughts and emotions without fear of judgment. Through their open communication, Karola has made debunking harmful stereotypes and misconceptions as well as issues of consent, healthy relationships, and equality, topics that are always on the table. Through her authentic guidance, she was able to model to her sons that true strength is not about dominance but about lifting others. As they continue to grow, she watches with pride as they make choices that reflect the values she has instilled.

She has had the privilege of witnessing the evolution of innocent toddlers into young men of integrity, character, and potential, finding herself growing alongside them in awe of her capacity for love.

Her parents, pillars of her life, would visit every time they could, watching their grandsons go through the different stages of life. This was new to them; having had four daughters, these playful, energetic boys brought a different kind of joy to their lives. When COVID-19 struck, Karola's parents were among the millions of people who were battling for their lives. With their fierce determination that stemmed from their unconditional love, she and her sisters did everything in their possibilities to help them in every way they could, balancing their own responsibilities and challenges.

As for many, the toll was not only emotional but financial. The medical bills and need for specialized care added to this extremely difficult time, yet together, as a team, they pooled their resources, both financial and emotional, and provided their parents with the care they deserved. Their sacrifices were a reflection of their parents' sacrifices for them throughout their lives, a heartfelt expression of gratitude and reciprocity. Together, they overcame the most difficult of times yet again.

Throughout these more than two decades, Karola has had different friendships and romantic relationships, some that were extremely positive and added to her life and story, and others, not so much. Her last romantic relationship is one that marked her in the most profound way.

It was a relationship that transcended the boundaries of distance, a connection so surreal that it seemed like a fairy tale. He was a man of kindness and depth who showered her with affection constantly, even if they lived miles apart. His gestures always spoke louder than his words, making her feel something she had never felt before. When they were together, the world seemed to fade into the background, with shared dreams and a profound sense of belonging neither had ever felt. Karola could not believe she had finally found what she had always been looking for in a partner. Their connection seemed somewhat magical, a type of unbreakable bond of two souls drawn together by fate.

They would text and talk constantly, sharing everyday trivialities as well as the most intimate details about their lives. They were always in touch, making the miles that separated them physically seem invisible. Their connection was something so extraordinary that it gives me shivers down my spine.

On any given September day, Karola was feeling worried; something seemed off. She texted him and received no answer. She knew he would be traveling, and maybe that was the reason she hadn't heard from him, but her intuition told her otherwise. Their connection, a vibrant lifeline, began to feel like a fragile thread. She got a phone call; he had been in an accident and lost his life. That afternoon, a bouquet of flowers with a beautiful note arrived from him on the day he lost his life, a testament to their unexplainable connection. As she held the flowers, she thought about how, even in death, he had shown her unconditional love. In the aftermath of such a painful loss, she is now the keeper of their love story and shares it with a sad smile. She knows she was extremely fortunate, for even if for a very short time, she experienced something many people don't experience in an entire lifetime.

Karola has experienced love and loss, freedom and slavery, emptiness and joy, doubt and faith, and all of these experiences have continued to contribute to the extraordinary human being she is. The light that emanates from her is a reflection of her spirit, making any person feel at home. I believe it comes from a depth of understanding that goes beyond what most of us can understand. It is amazing to me how, in her presence, conversations flow effortlessly, giving way to a sense of genuine connection. This light is constant and illuminates both her path and the paths of those of us who are fortunate enough to share in her presence. In a world that sometimes seems consumed by darkness, people who carry within them such intense luminosity that inspires and propels others to shift into a gratitude mindset are a gift. Karola is a gift.

Time has come and gone, leaving memories etched into the deepest parts of her being. She has been fortunate enough to witness that it is not exactly that time heals all wounds, but what we do with time as it goes by that helps us heal. With it being such an important part of her journey, healing has shown up in many different ways throughout her life, allowing her to develop even more compassion and the ability to offer solace to others who have gone through similar experiences. She has had the opportunity to travel, learn from many different people, have extraordinary relationships, and experience so much in such a short period. Without a doubt, her love and connection with her sons and with God are her fuel, and time has served her kindly, allowing her the gift of a broad and positive outlook on life itself, love, loss, gratitude, and every life encounter she experiences. She really is, without a doubt, an inspiration to all of us.

CHAPTER 27:
An Opinion

After countless hours of research, I can honestly say that I have my opinion on everything that happened. It is an opinion—like that of any other person, yet I can say, with my heart on my sleeve, that it got extremely confusing there for a while. I saw footage from the early 1990s until today. I read every article I was able to find...and I felt manipulated, confused, and somehow encouraged by the media to see things a certain way.

Everyone has an opinion, and everyone is entitled to one. Yet, as Harlan Ellison so eloquently said, "You are not entitled to your opinion. You are entitled to your informed opinion. No one is entitled to be ignorant." When it comes to having opinions about public figures/celebrities—we tend to go all out. Some people hide behind their screens, defending their celebrities as if they were family, and others are just along the ride to see the comments.

I used to have one of Laura's cassettes when I was a teenager. I know many of her songs by heart. Her irreverent, rebellious attitude made a thirteen-year-old living in the Mexican sexist society feel invincible. But it was all a lie, and sadly, my dear readers, it usually is.

I can have tons of opinions about people I have never met. Opinions pertaining to their art—in any form—to their abilities, to their looks... an opinion is something we can have due to freedom of speech. For me, social justice has always been an issue that I have felt extremely passionate about since a very early age, and knowing everything that happened to Karola makes my opinion a loaded one.

We have to remember that facts and opinions are different. A fact is verifiable, and we can determine whether it is true or not by researching the evidence. However, facts by themselves are worthless unless we put them in context, draw conclusions, and give them meaning. An opinion is a judgment based on facts, an honest attempt to draw a reasonable conclusion from factual evidence. An opinion is potentially changeable—

depending on how the evidence is interpreted, yet without facts, opinions have little power.[102]

I understand that opinions will be biased, yet I ask myself, how can we be biased toward a person who, whether victim at the beginning or not, groomed so many young women into that life, knowing exactly what she was leading them into, using herself as bait? I get it; she allegedly started down that path at fifteen years old, and much of her internal dialogue was molded by her surroundings. Yet, how incongruent is the fact that when in an interview you read earlier, the interviewer referred to the teenagers that were victims as young girls, and Laura corrected her, saying, "They are not young girls; they are birthed women" (the best translation I can come up with for *"señoras paridas"*). So, how exactly does it work? Does the physical and cognitive immaturity of a teenager only apply to her when it comes to being accountable?

Honestly, it makes me mad to actually like some of her songs... because I do; it conflicts me. It reminds me of my teenage years, singing them with my best friends as we prank-called the boys we liked. They bring me good memories. Then, I remember Karola and I are the same age, and while I was singing Laura's songs, dancing in my backyard, and feeling rebellious, Karola was being raped, starved, and obligated to perform forced labor...all because Laura got her there. So, at karaoke time nowadays, I don't necessarily always take the time to lecture the people around me about who Laura really is (particularly because it is not the time or place), but I do exit the room. It is my form of protest.

So, yes, I get it. When you are a fan, imagining your celebrity doing horrible things is not in the books, but we have to understand that, sometimes, what we see or want to see about our favorite celebrities has little or nothing to do with who they actually are.

So much footage, so much information, including a song from 1991 where, in 1999, they found a subliminal message. The beginning of the song has some type of gibberish, and when you play it backward, you can hear Antonio's voice saying, "That is why you must obey," a cryptic voice saying, "Punished," and Laura's voice saying, "You did it wrong."

---

102   "Distinguishing Fact, Opinion, Belief, and Prejudice." Writing@CSU, n.d. https://writing.colostate.edu/guides/teaching/co300man/pop12d.cfm#:~:text=-Facts percent20provide percent20crucial percent20support percent20for,reasonable percent20conclusion percent20from percent20factual percent20evidence.

CHAPTER 27: AN OPINION

When they questioned Antonio about this, he said he didn't remember, and then he said it was a joke of sorts. There are so many layers to this that besides the fact that it is incredibly confusing, it is incredibly disgusting and evil. Everything they did, and the way they did it, lacks basic humanity. I honestly cannot understand how things have played out the way they have.

All of the "he said, she said" led me to think of my dearest Johnny Depp, whom I've adored since *What's Eating Gilbert Grape, Crybaby, Ed Wood*, and let's not forget *Edward Scissorhands*. It was a bit of a struggle not to be manipulated by the media and the collective hate toward his ex-partner when, in my opinion, she was extremely unpleasant. But my handsome, adventurous, funny, talented Johnny Depp was violent, did contribute to his toxic relationship, and was under the influence of different substances during his time in that relationship, therefore having some of the responsibility for everything that went down. Of course, I was team Johnny. Are you kidding? Poor Johnny. He was attacked by his ex-partner, a gold digger hungry for fame....

And then, it dawned on me. Both of them contributed violently to their toxic relationship. *In this case*, it was a two-way street with everybody and their dog getting to have an opinion on the matter, many—many—rooting for Captain Jack Sparrow. Yet, in this case, we are talking about two consenting adults who were in a relationship by choice and ended up destroying it for many different reasons.

Do we actually know what really happened between them? No. Do we know if they actually adored each other at some point? No. We know what they allowed us to see from an open trial, and we have opinions influenced by the media.

I like to think of myself as an authentic person with independent opinions, and I'm extremely opinionated, that's for sure. Even when I try to be extremely mindful of my opinions, try to analyze them, and reflect on them, I get pulled into it all. I think we all do.

Now imagine the Johnny Depp scenario or any scenario with a public figure/celebrity.... Imagine people having an uninformed opinion about your life, about your parents, about your "fame-driven actions"...*when you were thirteen years old*.

It's kind of like the "she asked for it" for wearing a short skirt. It invalidates the torturous nightmare *many* young girls lived at the hands of these people, justifying the perpetrators because "we like them."

Yeah, I like Johnny Depp. I still think he's vitriolic, though, and his substance abuse, as well as his difficulties, make him very unstable. That doesn't mean he's not a great actor (in my opinion) and that he hasn't done amazing films.

Karola hasn't said much until now, twenty-four years later. She focused on raising her sons, creating a life of value for herself and her family, and surviving and working every single day to give her children everything she could. She went to live in a place where they wouldn't recognize her after her face was all over the magazines, newspapers, and TV shows. She built a simple, valuable life. Still, to this day, she has to hear about what happened to her from others, including Laura.

2018 Latin AMAs: ▇▇▇▇▇ **Talks MeToo Movement, Arrest in Emotional Speech**

Following her emotional speech, ▇▇ performed the equally emotional song, ▇▇▇▇▇

By Sofia Cerda Campero • Published October 26, 2018 • Updated on October 26, 2018 at 5:20 pm

Mexican superstar ▇▇▇▇ delivered a passionate speech about the MeToo Movement at Thursday night's Latin American Music Awards, revealing painful details of her past with a former producer that ultimately led to a stint in prison.

▇▇ served as co-host of the award show along with ▇▇▇ ▇▇, ▇▇▇, ▇▇▇ and ▇▇▇ She also premiered a new song, prefacing her performance by telling the audience about the unfortunate experiences she's endured over the years.

In the '90s, ▇▇ and ▇▇▇▇, her producer and mentor at the time, were accused of corrupting and abusing minors. She served four years in prison in connection to the scandal until her conviction was overturned in 2004.

"Those who don't know me and thus, don't like me, have probably heard millions of stories about me, among them, that I was in jail,"

███ told the audience. "Yes. It took the Mexican justice system four years, eight months and eight days to realize I was innocent. I was a smokescreen for the deaths in the city of Juárez, by condemning one woman you can conceal the crimes of others."

In her speech, ███ addressed her relationship with ███, who the ███ singer had at one time been romantically involved with. She also denied being his partner in crime.

███ explained she was only 15 years old when she met him and believed she needed him if she ever wanted to have a successful career. Slowly he began to manipulate her, she said, and accused him of beating and insulting her over a 17-year period.

"He was not my creator and he did not discover me because with or without him I have proven I am ███," she said to a roaring applause as audience members stood up.

███ explained she is only one of the many women ███ took advantage of, noting her oppressor is free and likely still hurting other women. She said that is because women who speak out against their abusers are often chastised instead of punishing the oppressor and called for an end to victim shaming.

The Mexican popstar finished her moving speech by saying:

"There are still people who discriminate me because they are ignorant. This has to end. I'm not saying this for me, I am fine. This has to end for them, so there is not a single woman in the world, who after facing her abuser, has to walk down the street being signaled by some idiot who accuses her of being a partner of her worst nightmare. Tonight I expose my life for them, because I am them," she said.

Following her emotional speech, ███ performed the equally emotional song, ███.

███ began her career in the late '80s. Widely known as the "Mexican Madonna," ███ big hair, leather vests, ragged tights and provocative attitude made her seem unstoppable. She sold 20 million records, starred in three hit films, and packed arenas worldwide in her 30-year career. Seen as sex symbol, her pin-up calendars sold millions.

In the late '90s, however, her career was tainted with scandals. She was accused in 1997 of helping ▇▇▇▇▇ brainwash young aspiring girls to turn them into sex slaves. ▇▇▇ was detained in 2000 while she was living in Brazil and spent three years in a Rio de Janeiro jail without being legally prosecuted. In 2002, she was extradited to Mexico where she was convicted of kidnapping and abuse of minors. She was released on Sept. 21, 2004 due to lack of evidence.[103]

Now, I don't know about you, but to me, this is ridiculous. The many childhoods/adolescences that were ruined by these people have value. She was not used as a scapegoat; she contributed to the situations that happened. Nobody "framed her" trying to create a diversion. Give me a break!

In another interview from the early 2000s, Laura talked about a particular young woman saying that if she was actually being starved, raped, and enslaved, how is it that if she had access to a microphone and the public, she didn't scream, "Help!"[104] She asked with a disgusting smirk. My instant thought of what I would reply to her was, "Why didn't you?" But since I am fortunate enough to have synapsis between my neurons, I would have never said anything like that, not even to her. Because I understand that when people are under severe manipulation and abuse, that does not seem like an option.

I get it. Sometimes, it's easier to target the patriarchy and toxic masculinity than it is to view individual situations for what they are. Do we all make mistakes? Without a doubt. Is it up to me or you to judge others for their mistakes? Unfortunately, as much as some of us enjoy judging other people, it is up to the justice system. Is the Mexican justice system corrupt? It couldn't be more crooked. Is it up to us to judge if Laura is actually a God-fearing person? No. Yet it is up to us to question ourselves and the situation and to try to learn from it.

In many of the countless videos taken of Laura throughout the

---

103   Campero, Sofia Cerda. "2018 Latin Amas: ▇▇▇▇ Talks Metoo Movement, Arrest in Emotional Speech." NBC New York, October 26, 2018. https://www.nbc-newyork.com/news/national-international/▇▇▇▇-2018-latin-american-music-awards-ellas-soy-yo/2064595/.
104   Candiani, Ana Patricia. "▇▇▇▇ Especial de Ocurrió Así." YouTube, January 18, 2021. https://www.youtube.com/watch?v=vLTf0ELN7m8&t=1424s.

years, excluding shows where she simulates being possessed by the devil as she sang a song she wrote herself, she portrays herself as a God-fearing Catholic woman who wears a cross around her neck and crosses herself before interviews.

It seriously bothers me when people use God as a scapegoat. Yes, I do believe God loves us all, but using God's name to confuse people, gain credibility, and take absolutely no responsibility for our own actions and how these might have affected the lives of others is, in my humble opinion, pure manipulation.

From my perspective, it doesn't really matter if you consider yourself religious (of any religion) or quote Bible verses. It doesn't really matter if you wear the symbol that represents your religion on a necklace around your neck. It matters even less if you lie through your teeth and take zero accountability for your actions. Growth of any kind, including spiritual growth, requires responsibility. We all make mistakes; it is part of the human condition, yet acknowledging our mistakes is the first step towards repairing any damage we cause—whether on purpose or without intent.

If we hide behind certain mannerisms or phrases to appear to be who we are not, to trick millions of people into believing "our side" of the story, then honestly, there really isn't much hope for growth. There are three versions to every story: yours, mine, and the actual truth. We each live our own truth and choose how to live our lives.

In my personal opinion, and it is just that, an opinion, Laura developed Stockholm syndrome, and as Paulo Freire so eloquently said, "The oppressed, instead of striving for liberation, tend themselves to become oppressors."

She was a victim turned victimizer, with fame and fortune at stake. She reeled girls in (key word in this sentence: girls); she knew what would happen to them, and she did it anyway. This is a crime. Mind you, in other interviews, both Laura and Antonio excuse the age of the girls by stating that Mexico stipulates what a minor is, in reference to what is or is not considered abuse, differently in different states. They stated several times that that is the reason they were tried in Chihuahua. Again...this seems like a bad joke. Rape is rape, abuse is abuse, slavery is slavery, a teenager is a teenager, and an adult is an adult. Consent does not happen through coercion, and it happens less through coercion with people in a position of power who are at least double your age. When we try to find loopholes like these to justify something so atrocious, like what happened to Karola and all the other teenagers, besides the fact that it is just evil, it is entirely absurd. I don't know if Laura did it so she would not suffer alone, or to feel a rush of power, or because of pain or cruelty…maybe because she was under Antonio's manipulation for so many years that she couldn't think clearly. I don't know; it really is impossible to.

What is shocking to me is that Jeffery Epstein was able to have a trial, as well as Guislaine Maxwell (who, in my opinion, did pretty much the same thing Laura did), yet Antonio and Laura "served" their time and got cleared of charges in a corrupt system when the human trafficking law had not even passed in Mexico.

It is not my place because I didn't live it, I am not part of the justice system, and I do not personally know them…yet I ask you this: Should Antonio currently be allowed to teach children music? Well, allegedly, he is. Should Laura be able to continue making money from this story, posing as a victim, when she was such a large part of the problem? Well, apparently, she is. Among many—many—things throughout the years, Laura made a TV series that aired in 2023 telling "her story" in which different actresses, using different names, portrayed the different young women involved in this "clan." Of course, someone played Karola, and from what I hear (I did not watch it, obviously), Karola's character was one of the meanest to Laura in the show. It is interesting to me to try to understand everything from many points of view, trying to understand how allegedly a thirteen-year-old could bully a twenty-eight-year-old pop star.

The countless—seriously countless—interviews I saw for research for this book made me feel sick. The lack of responsibility, arrogance, contradictions, incongruencies, and "tears" followed by rage, gaslighting, inconsistencies, manipulation, and blame-placing is revolting.

In March of 2023, a change.org petition to cancel Laura flooded Twitter. People are understanding, and others, her millions of fans, attack the victims. She has said she was so manipulated that she didn't realize what was going on, and in an interview from the early 2000s, when questioned about the different sexual abuse allegations, she laughed.[105] She said they should interview the other girls and ask them if anyone forced them, and if they didn't enjoy it, or if they didn't make sounds of enjoyment during sexual intercourse, implying with her words and body language that the underage girls who were forced to have intercourse with Antonio did it because they wanted to, and enjoyed it. First of all...how did she know what they sounded like while having intercourse? Second, the number of absurdities she has said throughout the years should be enough to make anyone see behind the countless masks she wears. The video footage anybody can find on YouTube of interviews throughout the past twenty years can make anyone see something is seriously off.

When confronted with the fact that Karola and her sister had Antonio's babies three months apart from each other and months apart from her (her daughter passed away a little over a month after she was born), she angrily replied they each had a relationship with Antonio before she did, and more importantly, that she didn't care. This interview is extraordinary, and although she might try to pass their situation as polyamory, you can see the hatred in her eyes. It doesn't take rocket science to figure it out, yet the fact that some people can't see it and attack the victims makes me furious. I don't understand. I seriously don't.

In another interview, Laura said, "In what head does the idea of being raped, starved, mistreated, without being famous fit? Then why did you continue? Can you explain it to me? Because I really don't understand. No, maybe in reality, you were very well-screwed, well-fed, hanging from the fortune and fame of someone else. ...I don't know in their case, but if any of them, be it an ex-wife or ex-lover, had sex with Antonio or with anyone because of an interest in wanting fame, then they are victims of their own ambition, and they have themselves to blame, and should look at themselves in the mirror. Because one gives their body and emotions for love, and if you do it for any other reason, then don't complain."[106]

This statement is from a woman who groomed a thirteen-year-old, telling her that private parts are just like any other parts of the body, that

105 ███████ Channel. "███████ / El Recuento de Los Daños (Documental Parte Del Capitulo 12)." YouTube, October 16, 2021. https://www.youtube.com/watch?v=tiDLVcKXrVU.
106 "███████ - Adela Micha - ███████ - Audio Mejorado." YouTube, November 5, 2022. https://www.youtube.com/watch?v=88ZrtMb_Gck.

sex is natural, not to have a small-town girl mentality, and to tell a man twenty-seven years older than her that she cares for him. From a woman who pulled a thirteen-year-old to a forty-one-year-old man's bedroom door, knocked, and ran away, leaving her there, and who would make her undress in front of her to then dress her up in lingerie.

In the same interview, Laura said she doesn't know what sex is; she has only made love. She grew up with her great-grandmother, who instilled in her the idea of the importance of virginity, so she lost her virginity much later, when she was eighteen years old, with her first boyfriend. She was then asked, "After that first boyfriend, how many others?" Her response...one.[107]

Interviewer, "The father of your daughter, may she rest in peace."

Laura, "Yes."

Interviewer, "Antonio?"

Laura, "Yes."

This might all sound believable, even if all of her actions implied otherwise. The reason I didn't believe it, although, for a brief moment, she seemed sincere, is due to another interview where she says, "If I could, I would make a law that just like boys get circumcised, they would take girls' virginity at birth, because women shouldn't be valued by a little tissue, we have more important things."[108]

So, dear readers.... The information is overwhelming and is a lot to analyze. Of course, in reference to the last paragraph, women are human beings who should be valued for who they are, and virginity has nothing to do with that. Yet, to be so contradictory and make such strong statements that, although it might have been with the intention of a feminist point of view, sounds more like female mutilation. I agree that virginity should not be considered the most important thing in anyone's life—yet that is up to every single person to decide how much value we put on that. Laura nor Antonio should have been able to make that decision for so many young women.

During one of my conversations with Karola, I told her, "I'm not sure

107 Ídem.
108 ████ Channel. "████ / El Recuento de Los Daños (Documental Parte Del Capitulo 12)." YouTube, October 16, 2021. https://www.youtube.com/watch?v=tiDLVcKXrVU.

what you are going to think of the book when you read it. I know what you want me to portray is how love and faith are what saved you, but I'm just so angry."

As sweet as she always is, we had a long conversation about this. She said anger doesn't rule her heart anymore, but she understands how when people actually understand what happened, they feel angry, frustrated, and extremely discouraged with the justice system, with the music industry, with the media...and just generally with the human race.

Some people have said Laura was able to be cleared from charges because of "insufficient evidence" because she had links with mafia lord "Señor de los Cielos," who pretty much made her immune to anything. Others have said she made a pact with Satan (there are some videos in the early '90s that might make anyone think that), there are other people who think she is mentally ill, and others who believe she is just plain evil. Some believe she was a victim of Antonio and had nothing to do with the fact that the underage girls who ended up in their care, being exploited and tortured, were promised a music career using her as an example. I know what I believe, and I could go on and on, but this book isn't about that.

CHAPTER 28:
2023

The year in which Prince Harry's book *Spare* was published, Tom Brady (actually) retired, Harvey Weinstein was sentenced, FBI Director Christopher Wray confirmed the bureau believes COVID-19 pandemic likely originated from a lab accident in Wuhan, China, "Flowers" of Miley Cyrus was everywhere, the movie *Sound of Freedom* came out, and the year I met Karola, billboards of Laura's concerts were all over Mexico City. At the beginning of the year, an article in Rolling Stone came out that said,

> Nearly two decades after a judge abruptly cleared pop diva ███ of charges she lured minors into a secret sex ring in Mexico, the singer is facing a new civil lawsuit in Los Angeles that revives claims she procured underage girls for her ex-producer ███.
>
> The new complaint, obtained by Rolling Stone, was filed shortly before the Dec. 31 deadline for a three-year "lookback" window that temporarily lifted the statute of limitations on childhood sex assault claims in California. Neither ███ nor ███ are specifically named in the suit, but it's clear they're the top two Doe defendants based on details including concerts ███ played in the 1990s and albums she recorded.
>
> According to the filing, two Jane Doe plaintiffs allege they were 13 and 15 years old respectively when ███ approached them in public and lured them into joining ███ purported music training program by promoting it as an elite star-making opportunity. The victims says ███ groomed them to become sex slaves to ███, and that much of their abuse happened in Los Angeles County.
>
> By the time the Jane Does were recruited, ███ and ███ already had reached international fame with a series of hits showcasing ███ edgy lyrics and rebellious persona, the lawsuit states. ███ was dubbed Mexico's version of Madonna while ███ was credited as her behind-the-scenes production ace. It would be several years before the once-celebrated duo would seemingly disappear ahead of a flood of sex cult allegations from multiple former

protégées. The claims would explode into an international scandal, with ███████ painted as a violent serial pedophile and ███ as his willing accomplice. The two would be arrested in Brazil in January 2000 after an international manhunt.

███████, now 54, spent four years in pre-trial detention but was ultimately acquitted when a judge said there was insufficient evidence to support the rape, kidnapping and corruption of minors' charges filed against her by Mexican prosecutors. After spending four years awaiting trial, ████████ was convicted of rape, kidnapping and corruption of minors, but ended up spending only one more year behind bars.

Jane had something to say about this...

The article that came out in the newspaper "La Jornada de Enmedio" on August 11, 2023, says the following,

> The singer Jane presented a civil lawsuit against two people who accused her of having participated in the crime of sexual abuse, and the complaint includes the producer, Antonio. In the lawsuit, Jane reveals that since 2021, she had a meeting with an FBI agent who asked for information about Antonio, considering her the first victim of the producer.
>
> Sources close to the case said that in her lawsuit, Jane evidenced the FBI investigates the activities of the so-called clan.[109]

"La Jornada" possesses a copy of the lawsuit presented to the Court of Glendale, California, in which Antonio is signaled as "an adult man, known and successful Mexican music producer who was sentenced for rape, kidnapping, and corruption of minors, for almost eight years."

According to journalistic records, in March 2005, the seventh criminal court of the state of Chihuahua declared Antonio guilty of the crimes of corruption of minors, kidnapping, and aggravated rape. He was sentenced to seven years and ten months in prison and ordered to pay a fine equivalent

---

109 Castillo, Gustavo. "███████████ Demanda En California a Dos Personas Que La Acusan de Abuso Sexual." La Jornada, August 11, 2023. https://www.jornada.com.mx/2023/08/11/espectaculos/a08n2esp.

to 3,591 pesos, as well as 1,061,500 pesos for the moral damage caused to the minor. Jane stated to the court that she was married to Antonio "when she was fifteen years old, from 1985–1990," and they divorced in order for her to marry another of the defendants, identified by a codename.

In her lawsuit, the singer mentioned that around December 2021, one of the defendants in her case, who also filed a civil lawsuit against Antonio, contacted her and informed her of their intentions to take Antonio to US courts for child abuse. During this encounter, one of Antonio's victims introduced her to two lawyers, and later, an FBI agent was introduced to her. The FBI agent mentioned that she should join the lawsuit against the talent manager "as the first victim of the criminal Antonio and the one who endured his regime for the longest time." Jane stated in her account that she responded to the victim and the FBI agent that she would think about it and get in touch with them later due to her health conditions, as she didn't want to go through further traumas.

After this encounter, Jane mentioned that both Antonio's victim and the FBI agent became more insistent through phone calls and messages, urging her to become one of the plaintiffs. However, she did not participate in the lawsuit against the artistic producer. The examination of Jane's lawsuit is under the jurisdiction of Judge Ralph C. Hoffer. In her statement, the singer claims compensation, asserting that everything she has experienced, as well as the lawsuit filed against her in December by two victims of sexual abuse involving Laura and Antonio, have led her to be defamed and to suffer emotional distress.

Justice is decided by the justice system, and although everyone has their version of what happened, there are several things that can't be denied. In Karola's case, the fact that she was a minor who was groomed, coerced, manipulated, enslaved, starved, and raped—by people who were adults is crystal clear. Although most of the women who were involved in this scandal arrived with Laura and/or Antonio when they were minors, the changing narratives of some have made public opinion extremely divided as to what actually happened. It is extremely difficult to know what is in the hearts and minds of others and what the intentions are that drive them to say and do whatever it is they choose to.

Yet we must understand that this is much bigger than the individual cases; this is about human trafficking, coercion, manipulation, and deceit...that occurred in front of the public eye without anyone noticing.

This is about understanding profoundly that these types of situations are not uncommon and that human trafficking is such a lucrative crime that many—many—people, very high up, all over the world, are involved.

That same summer, the movie *Sound of Freedom* came out. The film had a significant impact on me, as it conveyed reality without sensationalism, and it's gratifying to see this issue gaining more attention.

The shelters I had the privilege to know, such as *Fundación Camino a Casa* and *Comisión Unidos Contra la Trata*, are exceptional places. The love, preparation, kindness, empathy, passion, and dedication in these spaces are awe-inspiring.

Witnessing this firsthand and meeting the girls and boys—some rescued as young as four years old—from slavery and exploitation changes anyone's perspective on life. The care they receive with such affection, reminding them to put on lotion after bathing, fills my heart. These shelters provide education, psychological support, medical care, emotional comfort, love, and nutritious food—an unending labor of love that is difficult to comprehend.

Some of the survivors I've worked with in therapy arrived at the shelters as minors. Some had children as a result of rape, while others had severe emotional damage that led to a period of selective mutism.

Although it gives me hope that the issues of human trafficking and child pornography are finally receiving greater attention, there are some points I'd like to address:

1. We've made significant progress in the last two decades in raising awareness, education, laws, consciousness, and information about trafficking. The most critical aspect is the focus on survivors—as the United Nations states, "In the fight against human trafficking, let survivors lead the way." Tim Ballard is undoubtedly a hero, just like Schindler was, and people like them provide hope. But to truly understand trafficking, we must listen to the voices of the victims, who sadly comprise only 2 percent of survivors.

2. The movie mostly takes place in Colombia, but human trafficking is a global crime, with more victims than the population of Canada. Mexico ranks third in human trafficking, following closely behind Thailand and Cambodia. In terms of child pornography production and distribution, Mexico holds the first place. It's essential to

remember that trafficking takes various forms, including sexual exploitation, forced labor, forced begging, and even illegal organ trafficking and biomedical experimentation. There have been investigations and dismantling of child pornography networks in Mexico for decades, so it's crucial to conduct thorough research.

3. While the movie aims to transmit hope and the possibility of healing, it's essential to understand the reality. Children arriving at shelters are often deeply traumatized, and it takes considerable collective effort and time to see them smile again.

4. Perpetrators of these crimes don't always fit the stereotypical image of "evil." Many may have jobs where they interact with children daily. We need to recognize the reality and be vigilant. The involvement of women in trafficking and grooming should not be underestimated. They can also be responsible for these heinous crimes.

5. There are many people doing good work to make a difference in the lives of victims and survivors. We can all contribute to positive change through increased awareness and conscious actions in our daily lives, such as being mindful of the products we buy.

When I saw the movie, I obviously thought of Karola. I also thought of many of the survivors I know and care about. This is not the world we want to live in, and it is up to us to be the change we want to see. As Jim Caviezel said in the movie, "God's children are not for sale," and dear readers, we are all God's children.

> For everything there is a season, a time for every activity under heaven. A time to be born and a time to die. A time to plant and a time to harvest. A time to kill and a time to heal. A time to tear down and a time to build up. A time to cry and a time to laugh. A time to grieve and a time to dance. A time to scatter stones and a time to gather stones. A time to embrace and a time to turn away. A time to search and a time to quit searching. A time to keep and a time to throw away. A time to tear and a time to mend. A time to be quiet and a time to speak. A time to love and a time to hate. A time for war and a time for peace.
>
> Ecclesiastes 3:1–8 (NLT)

CHAPTER 29:
Gratitude

Karola lives a grateful life. She has told me several times that what she is most grateful for is her sons and having God in her life. She practices gratitude in every way she can, and one of the most astonishing ways she does this is by being the international president of Comisión Unidos Contra la Trata. Her altruism, faith, gratitude, love, and light give back to those who need it the most. She takes care of herself because she knows how important it is for her to live her best life, yet she is always thinking of others. Her kindness, sense of humor, charisma, empathy, and inclusiveness make her a key person for combating human trafficking.

We have had several conversations about the impact and advantages of gratitude and how it helps us shift our perspective and be centered in a growth mindset. Many studies over the past decade have discovered that people who consciously acknowledge their blessings tend to experience greater happiness and reduced levels of depression. Without a doubt, gratitude has an important impact on our mental health.

Dr. Robert A. Emmons from the University of California, Davis, and Dr. Michael E. McCullough from the University of Miami have conducted extensive research on the subject of gratitude. In a particular study, they instructed participants to write a few sentences every week focusing on specific topics. One group was asked to write about things they were thankful for that had occurred during the week. A second group documented daily annoyances or displeasing experiences, while the third group wrote about events that had impacted them without any emphasis on their positivity or negativity. After a span of ten weeks, those who wrote about gratitude displayed greater optimism and an improved outlook on life. Interestingly, they also engaged in more physical exercise and had fewer visits to doctors compared to those who dwelled on sources of irritation.[110]

Another prominent researcher in this field, Dr. Martin E. P. Seligman, a psychologist at the University of Pennsylvania, conducted a study involving 411 individuals. Each participant was assigned a positive psychology

---

110 "Giving Thanks Can Make You Happier." Harvard Health Publishing, August 14, 2021. https://www.health.harvard.edu/healthbeat/giving-thanks-can-make-you-happier.

intervention, with a control group writing about early memories. When the task involved writing and personally delivering a gratitude letter to someone who had never received proper appreciation for their kindness, the participants experienced a significant surge in their happiness scores. This effect exceeded the impact of any other intervention, and its benefits endured for a month.

Naturally, studies such as these cannot definitively establish a causal relationship, yet most of the research conducted in this area supports a connection between gratitude and an individual's overall well-being. Additional investigations have explored how practicing gratitude can enhance relationships. While research generally showcases the positive effects of gratitude, there are always some exceptions that might suggest that gratitude may be an achievement linked to emotional maturity.[111]

With exceptions or not, we have felt the effects of gratitude in our lives and know that when we feel it genuinely, it's as if a veil with the heaviness of some of our experiences has been lifted. Gratitude gives us the possibility to view everything around us and within us with a certain type of philosophy. We can cultivate our gratitude on a regular basis through appreciation for our loved ones and God. We can make a habit out of it and live thankfully. We are blessed, and counting our blessings will help us stay attuned to what actually matters to us.

I am profoundly grateful to know Karola. I am immensely grateful to have the honor and opportunity to tell her story because when we immerse ourselves in the world of human trafficking, we feel all the feelings, and believe me, gratitude is not one that is normally present.

Both Karola and I are grateful to you, dear readers, for embarking on this journey with us. For feeling the sadness, the anger, the love, the faith, the relief, the impotence, and the joy of the story these pages hold within them. Thank you for being brave enough to take the time to learn about Karola's story and about what human trafficking is. Together is the only way we can really make a difference.

I finish this book, dear readers, with Karola's words that she shared with me while on an extraordinary contemplative experience she had. I hope through her own words, you can get a sense of the astonishing beauty, resilience, and light Karola encompasses as a human being.

---

111 Ídem.

CHAPTER 29: GRATITUDE

I always tell her I admire her profoundly, not because she overcame what happened to her, but because of who she is in spite of everything.

Today is the day of restitution, of all the days of all the years of all the lives in which I have not received justice, care, security, a hug, a solution, and an opportunity to live in safety.

It is the day to completely turn to a new reality, a paradigm shift from the information I received in which no one was there for me.

The thief comes to kill, steal, and destroy, but God comes to give me life and life abundantly.

Today, I humbly receive everything that, until yesterday, I had to give to myself, and not only to myself but to others as well. I no longer have to rebel against a system that abandoned me!

Today, I receive protection, care, and reparation for the damage.

Today, I feel in my place and I feel secure, and that eternal knot in my throat can begin to dissolve.

I receive all the love, support, understanding, and apologies from an entire universe that was not there for me. Today, I receive the restitution of seventy times seven for everything that was stolen from me, for the life that was taken from me, and for everything I had to overcompensate for, to forget that I was a child and had to take care of myself and my babies.

Today, I conclude that study, the thesis of a life in which I studied how to understand everything that did not understand me, and I graduate having done the best I could, undoubtedly with a lot of love. Thank You, Lord. I am ready for my graduation.

Karola pictured in 2023 at a UN conference.

EPILOGUE

As I sit down to pen this epilogue, I am reminded of the journey that led me here—the countless hours of contemplation, the exhilarating highs of inspiration, and the inevitable lows of disappointment while being a witness to the evolution of one of the most beautiful friendships I have ever had. Writing is, many times, a solitary endeavor, but it is also a deeply communal one. In this particular book, it has taken a village. A village of wonderful people with the same objective: to combat human trafficking.

We have worked tirelessly together, each of us from the depths of our respective trenches, from reflecting on a difficult journey, digging into the past and remembering the most difficult moments, to poring over data, researching, listening actively, and connecting the dots, that although connected many times before, continue to be dissected through the media at the convenience of others.

Together, we have weaved this project in the most heavenly-guided way, converting the collection of words strung together into a testament to the power of faith, resilience of the human spirit, and love.

We release these words into the world with our hearts full of love and faith. We believe in being the change we want to see in the world, even in one that is at times shrouded in darkness, because we know that through unity and solidarity, even the most insidious of evils can be overcome.

As with most things in life, it does take a village, and now, dear readers, you are part of it. To every one of you holding this book in your hands, we offer our sincerest gratitude. It is our hope that within these pages, you will find inspiration, you will feel our intention to contribute toward prevention, and you will join us in our battle to combat human trafficking.

May we stand together in solidarity, united in our commitment to end exploitation and injustice. And may we continue to build a world where every person is valued, cherished, and free to live their lives with dignity and grace.

Thank you for being part of the village,
—Raquel.

AFTERWORD

Karo,

About a decade ago, I received a message from God written in Acts 18:9–10 (paraphrased by the author),

> Then the Lord said to Paul in the night by a vision, "Do not be afraid, but speak, and do not keep silent; for I am with you, and no one will attack you to harm you; for I have many people in this city."

At that moment, I couldn't believe that God was asking me to do something that was impossible for me to do. The fear I always had of those I consider responsible for the serious events we lived through was too much. I knew there was a huge economic, political, and media power at play against which I could not compete. Additionally, the certainty of living in a country that never intended to protect us and a society that was not ready to listen paralyzed me. However, over time, I came to understand that it wasn't just about me or us but about delivering a message that could help bring so many stories out of the darkness, stories that have remained stuck in the hearts and throats of so many victims. Because even up to 99.9 percent of cases of sexual violence against adult women are never reported, what can we expect then from abuses against children and adolescents? But there's a reason we are alive, and we couldn't let this opportunity pass to transform our story into a greater purpose. That's how, as time has passed, I have been able to understand more and more each day the gravity of what we lived through and how Mexico, our country, decided to reduce it to a stack of papers in a bulging file when it is actually a brutal criminal case involving all kinds of abuses, exploitation, torture, and slavery, a case that not only Mexico but other countries like Brazil, Spain, Chile, and Argentina decided to archive. It cannot be ignored that no person, regardless of age or gender, should ever experience such terrible violations of human rights, but it also cannot be minimized that there were girls as young as you, and I feel it in my soul. I sincerely hope that fewer and fewer people will ignore us and reduce our pain to a mere media scandal. I hope that your voice sounds and resonates as far as it needs to go so that no child, young person, or teenager is ever robbed of their dreams again so that their wings are never clipped. Because confusion, lies, and injustice will never be the will of God. That's why order, truth, and justice are a reflection that God has decided to fight our battle. And against that, there is no one and nothing stronger.

With love,
Your sister Karla.

Karla de la Cuesta is a lawyer and lecturer with various diplomas in human trafficking, abolitionist leadership against sexual exploitation, and certification in trauma care, among others. She began her activism against these crimes in late 2012, and in 2015, she founded Alas Abiertas, a non-governmental organization where she has worked on prevention, training, and awareness-raising for authorities, legislative advocacy, and support for survivors of human trafficking. Her efforts have been recognized with distinctions such as the Humanize Award for the Defense of Human Rights by CODHEM in 2019, the Medal of Merit in Defense of Victims 2020 by the Mexico City Congress, and Recognition in 2023 as an outstanding inhabitant of Puebla in the Defense of Human Rights by the Presidency of the Board of the Senate of the Republic, among others. Her voice has been heard not only in Mexican forums but also internationally in countries such as Spain, Belgium, Switzerland, Guatemala, the United States, etc.

RESOURCES

Collaboration with survivor-led organizations and a survivor-centered approach is crucial to ensure the most effective support and empowerment of survivors. https://kaleidoinc.org/

CHILD PORNOGRAPHY

To report an incident involving the possession, distribution, receipt, or production of child pornography, file a report on the National Center for Missing & Exploited Children (NCMEC) website at www.cybertipline.com or call 1-800-843-5678. Your report will be forwarded to a law enforcement agency for investigation and action.

If you have an emergency that requires an immediate law enforcement response, please call 911 or contact your local police department or sheriff's department.

CHILD SEX TRAFFICKING

To report an incident or suspicious situation that may involve child sex trafficking, call the National Human Trafficking Resource Center (NHTRC) at 1-888-3737-888 or file a confidential online report at https://humantraffickinghotline.org/report-trafficking. Your report will be forwarded to a law enforcement agency for investigation and action.

If you have an emergency that requires an immediate law enforcement response, please call 911 or contact your local police department or sheriff's department.

CHILD SEXUAL ABUSE

Child sexual abuse matters are generally handled by local and state authorities and not by the federal government.

To report an incident or suspicious situation that may involve child sexual abuse, contact your local police department or sheriff's department.

If you have an emergency that requires an immediate law enforcement response, please call 911.

CHILD SUPPORT ENFORCEMENT

Child support enforcement matters are generally handled by local and state authorities and not by the federal government. To report a child support enforcement issue, contact your local or state law enforcement agency or contact your local "Title IV-D" agency, which is required by federal law to provide child support enforcement services to anyone who requests such services. To locate your local "Title IV-D" agency, visit the US Department of Health and Human Services, Office of Child Support Enforcement's website at http://www.acf.hhs.gov/css/parents.

EXTRATERRITORIAL SEXUAL EXPLOITATION OF CHILDREN

To report an incident or suspicious situation that may involve the extraterritorial sexual_exploitation of children, file a report on the National Center for Missing & Exploited Children (NCMEC) website at www.cybertipline.com or call 1-800-843-5678. Your report will be forwarded to a law enforcement agency for investigation and action.

You can also report an incident or suspicious situation to Immigration and Customs Enforcement/Homeland Security Investigations (ICE) by calling the ICE hotline at 1-866-347-2423 or submitting an ICE online tip form at https://www.ice.gov/webform/ice-tip-form.

INTERNATIONAL PARENTAL KIDNAPPING

To report an international parental kidnapping situation, contact the US Department of State, Office of Children's Issues at 1-888-407-4747 or 202-501-4444. You may also wish to visit the US Department of State International Parental Child Abduction website for information.

If you have an emergency that requires an immediate law enforcement response, please call 911 or contact your local police department or sheriff's department.

OBSCENITY

To report obscene material sent to a child, a misleading domain name, or misleading words or images on the internet, file a report on the National Center for Missing and Exploited Children (NCMEC) website at www.cybertipline.com or call 1-800-843-5678. Your report will be forwarded to a law enforcement agency for investigation and action.

To file a complaint about obscene or indecent material broadcast over the radio or television, contact the Federal Communication Commission (FCC) Consumer Complaint Center online at https://consumercomplaints.fcc.gov/hc/en-us or by calling the FCC at 1-888-CALL-FCC (1-888-225-5322).

SEX OFFENDER REGISTRATION

To report a non-compliant or unregistered sex offender, contact the United States Marshals Service (USMS) at https://www.usmarshals.gov/what-we-do/fugitive-investigations/submitting-a-tip.

ABOUT THE AUTHOR

Raquel Caspi is a Mexican-American psychologist, author, and anti-human trafficking activist. Born in Mexico City in 1982, Raquel has a bachelor's degree in human communication disorders. She has certifications in neurolinguistic programming, clinical psychology, and psychopathology, as well as positive psychology and human trafficking. She is also certified in neuropsychoeducation and transgenerational therapy. Raquel has a master's degree in transpersonal psychology and a PhD in human development. She has designed and implemented courses on personal development, ethics, and entrepreneurship. Raquel facilitates workshops on topics such as self-esteem, emotional intelligence, and sexual abuse prevention. Her research interests include mental health and resilience after trauma.

Printed in the USA
CPSIA information can be obtained
at www.ICGtesting.com
CBHW071629150824
13132CB00048B/714

9 798893 333695